TABLE OF COI

C000130589

ACKNOWLEDGEMENTS

Pierre-André Dubois, retired Master-Brewer, Past President of *Les Amis de la Bière* and font of knowledge on *la culture brassicole* has been always kind and helpful, often inspirational. Many thanks also to Philippe Bonnet, Philippe Brillon, , Yves Castelain, Eliane De Clerck, Alain Dhaussy, Gaston Dubois, Paul Edwards, Fabrice Gaudé, Chris Mercier, Louis Peugniez, the Ricour family, Pascal Segier, Claudie Seminet, the Theillier family, Philippe Voluer, and Monsieur and Madame Windels-Desprer.

Work in progress on this book appeared at various times in What's Brewing, France and Living France, so thank you to Roger Protz, Ted Bruning, Philip Faiers, Jon Stackpool, Trevor and Susan Yorke. From the North of England to the North of France, the only way to travel is Hull to Zeebrugge; thanks to Tony Farrell of P & O North Sea Ferries.

My wife, Jean Taylor, kept the show on the road and co-ordinated the production with exemplary skill and patience – heartfelt thanks and much love.

Dans la Tradition   DEPUIS 1885   Bière de Garde

Author: Arthur Taylor
Published by CAMRA Books, Campaign for Real Ale,
230 Hatfield Road, St Albans AL1 4LW
Tel: 01727 867201 Fax: 01727 867670
Design: Linda Rodgers, Flying Pig Design
Cover design: Mckie Associates
Illustrations: Linda Rodgers and Beverly Curl
Managing Editor: Mark Webb

ISBN 1-85249-140-X

© CAMRA Books 1998

Great effort has gone into researching the contents of this book, but no responsibility can be taken for errors.

INTRODUCTION

Northern France is beer-lovers' country, let there be no doubt about that. There are twenty-three breweries in the Nord-Pas de Calais, one in the neighbouring *département* of the Somme and another in Aisne – and there are more on the way as the idea of micro-breweries takes hold. *La Feuille de Houblon*, the national French trade magazine, estimated in 1997 that there were 70 breweries in the whole of the country, so on that reckoning, the North has well over a third of the total.

Between them, the Northern breweries produce a range of around seventy five *bières de dégustation*, a broad description, which translates as carefully crafted beers worth savouring, pondering and talking about. (A *bière de soif*, on the other hand, is a thirst-quencher, nothing more, nothing less. The phrase would cover most of the beers available on tap in most of the bars in France).

Most of the breweries sell at the door, many of them, if they are given advance notice, welcome visitors to look around. Expeditions to track down the regional beers at source would take you all over Northern France, from bustling ports like Calais to quiet, beautiful and almost unknown rural villages in French Flanders; from Lille, one of the liveliest cities in Europe, to the peaceful Roman town of Bavay; from the old coal-mining districts, the Basin Minier, to the tranquil, lazy waters of the Somme.

On the way, you will realise, if you are travelling the region for the first time, or if on previous trips, you have just passed through on the way somewhere else, what a diverse, fascinating and rewarding part of the world this is – and you will find that the beers, in their wide variety of styles, and flavours, reflect that diversity. You will learn a little regional history as well, when you query some of the names of the beers – La Bavaisienne, La Bière des Sans Culottes, La Choulette, Saison St-Médard, Hommelpap, L'Atrébate, Pot Flamand, Septante-

Cinq, Ch'Ti. You will be introduced, incidentally, but importantly, to traditional games, windmills, bell-towers and carillons, town and village fêtes, carnival giants, hop-fields, abandoned coal mines and miraculously transformed slag-heaps, genièvre (gin) and regional cheeses – all distinctive parts of Northern identity.

Beer culture remains strong. There are celebrations each year when the Special Spring beers, the *bières de Mars* arrive. These are only available from the 1st to the 31st March. In November, all the bars announce not only that the Beaujolais Nouveau is in stock, but that *la bière de Noël est arrivée!* – all the breweries, large and small, produce a special strong, warming Christmas beer, on sale through the festive season. There are great debates each year as to which of these winter warmers is the best, most interesting of the season.

In August/September, there are tours of the hop fields (and the cafés, bars and estaminets) of French Flanders, to mark the beginning and the end of the harvest. Many of the region's most hectic celebrations – the *Carnaval* in Dunkirk in February, the *Fête des Rats* in Arras in May, the *Grandes Fêtes de Gayant* at Douai in July, the *Grande Braderie* at Lille in September and the *Fête de Houblon* at Steenvoorde in October, feature beer, in quantity and quality, among the attractions and diversions on offer.

If you know where to look – and this guide should help – you can find bars, cafés, brasseries, tavernes and estaminets, which sell beers from the region (as well as beers from nearby Belgium). The new generation of estaminets and tavernes in Flanders, centres of hearty eating and drinking, folk music and traditional games, have to be experienced to be believed. French supermarkets in the North now invariably include a *cave à bière*, a corner devoted to regional beers – all you need is a checklist of the more interesting buys. You will find that list here.

Many restaurants include *cuisine à la bière* on their menus – you are much more likely to find, for example, *coq à la bière*, than *coq au vin*. A *carbonade*

Flamande will be enriched with beer (and maybe a spot of *genièvre*, or gin, another regional speciality). You might find some surprises – *oeufs pochés à la bière blonde* (eggs poached in pale ale), or *Le Welsh Rarebit*, made with beer.

Quite recently, the Association des Brasseurs de France produced a pamphlet extolling the virtues of "Bière et Mer" – the marriage of sea-food and beer. The restaurants along the North French coast knew all about that already. Philippe Olivier, the world famous cheese master, whose shop in Boulogne has long been on the "must visit" list of discerning British visitors, is working on a new book about the cheeses of Northern France, and there is to be a section suggesting which local beer will go best with which local cheese.

Les Amis de la Bière formed in 1986, are, as their name suggests, fond of their beer, especially if it comes from the North. They organise beer tastings, seminars on beer history and culture, fairs for collectors of breweriana and visits to breweries at home (ie in the north of France) and abroad (Belgium and Germany). The official launch of *les bières de Noël* is masterminded, in a different French town every year, by *Les Amis* and the *Syndicat des Brasseurs de la Region du Nord de la France*. Tickets are like gold dust. *Les Amis* produce a small but informative quarterly journal called *La Gazette des Eswards* and are affiliated to the European Beer Consumers' Union, as are De Objective Bierproevers (OBP), of Belgium, Promotie Informatie Traditioneel Bier (PINT), of Holland, and of course, The Campaign for Real Ale (CAMRA), of Great Britain.

Within their organisation, *Les Amis* have a militant wing, the *Ghilde des Eswards Cervoisiers*, who dress up in mediaeval uniform of robes, caps and sashes, together with a badge of office – a miniature beer barrel on a ribbon around the neck – and dash about the country and abroad as caped crusaders on behalf of their region's products, manning stalls at fairs and exhibitions, enrolling local dignitaries into the ranks, giving out the word to local newspapers and television stations. They are in no way unusual, for they function exactly as do other guilds and fraternities in France, but instead of wine, or sausages, or cheese, they defend and glorify their local beer.

This book could only have been compiled with a little help from my friends, *Les Amis de la Bière*, and members of the *Ghilde des Eswards*. The tour, I promise you, reaches the parts that other beers don't reach.

THE SHOCKING HISTORY OF BREWING IN NORTHERN FRANCE

The place for an overview of the history of brewing and beer in France is *La musée européen de la Bière* at Stenay, between Sedan and Verdun, in the Meuse. Here, you can work your way through the exhibits and the wall charts and follow the story of beer, world wide, from Ancient Egypt to the present day. In the mid-nineteenth century, Stenay marked an invisible frontier in France, between the early-industrialised breweries in Alsace and Lorraine, which, influenced by Austrian and German example, made bottom-fermented lagers, and the generally smaller brewers in Belgium and Northern France, who stuck by and large to their tradition of top-fermented beers. In the museum, you will be introduced to French heroes of brewing – Pasteur, of course, a key figure in the understanding of the fermentation process – but others as well, whose names are less familiar – Jean-Louis Baudelot, Eugene Velten. In the *Centre de Documentation* of the museum, there are impressive archives, where scholars of *la culture brassicole* can plunge into much more detailed research on individual breweries and their history.

What follows is not especially scholarly, but is simply a brisk scamper through the recent history of brewing in the Nord-Pas de Calais:

Gambrinus France are the national association of breweriana collectors. They buy, sell and exchange beer-mats and glasses or mugs, bottles and labels, smaller items of brewery equipment, trays and towels, ashtrays, advertising material, post cards and printed matter – anything and everything to do with long-gone (and not so long-gone) breweries. A reading of their quarterly magazine, *La Tegesto Gazette*, or a visit to one of their regular *bourse d'echanges* is an education in brewery history.

The Northern branch of Gambrinus has a lot of history to delve into. In 1939, well within living memory, there were just short of a thousand breweries in action in the Nord-Pas de Calais – in 1890 the same region had almost *two* thousand. Today, there are just over 20. To lose a thousand breweries is unfortunate – to lose two thousand begins to sound like carelessness, but there are reasons.

The First World War cut an immense swathe of destruction across the area; the front line of years of trench warfare and artillery bombardments ran through or near places like Bailleul, Béthune, Arras, and Peronne, while there were savage battles around Lens, Cambrai and St-Quentin. Breweries behind the German front line, which were not obliterated, were methodically pillaged by the invaders, who sent valuable materials, especially steel, pipework and non-ferrous metals such as copper, back to the Fatherland to aid the war effort. Among the large collection of postcards of destruction which were produced at the end of the war, besides the skeletal blackened remains of cathedrals, churches, châteaux, towns and villages, there were grainy black and white images of devastated breweries – these latter much prized today by the collectors of Gambrinus France.

The centres of the larger, more ancient and important towns were lovingly and painstakingly reconstructed as closely as possible to hold historic designs, often helped by international funds. The hôtel de ville, belfrey, main squares and arcades of Arras, to offer one famous example, look as if they have been there for centuries – they are all 1930s reconstructions. Smaller, less important towns and villages were rebuilt too, but in utilitarian (and imported) red brick and slate.

There was money available to rebuild businesses – reparations, or *dommages de guerre*, sometimes money, sometimes materials, extracted from defeated Germany. The process was long and torturous and many gave up their rightful claim to a share of the spoils through sheer frustration, or though lack of influential contacts. Many small brewers on agricultural property, who were successful in their claims, gave up brewing and invested the money on their farms. It was not just a question of rebuilding, but of re-thinking and expensive re-equipping – people set in their ways could not cope with new ideas such as steam power, electricity, refrigeration and bottling plants, deliveries by lorry instead of by horse and cart. Many were loath to abandon top-fermentation and yeasts and processes which they understood, for the new fashion of bottom-fermented Pils-style lagers, which required long periods of artificial refrigeration, but which nevertheless were becoming more and more popular.

A curious sociological effect of the war – many ex-combatant survivors from the beer-drinking Nord-Pas de Calais picked up the wine habit during their period of service, when they were issued with a daily ration of rough *vin rouge*. They looked for the same thing when they arrived home. It was the first crack in the hitherto universal beer-drinking habits of the North.

A few breweries, on the allied side of the lines and out of range of bombardment, most in the Pas-de-Calais, had done well. The brewery of St-Sylvestre, near Cassel, encouraged by locally-based British troops, even tried brewing stout, using torrified malts. The results, noted the brewery historian, were "catastrophique". Others, after the war, introduced stouts, porters and Scotch ales, directly influenced by the drinking habits of the departed British soldiery. Some of them linger on, even today.

Some adventurous souls, as we shall see, saw the opportunity to modernise, or build new breweries on the ruins of the old. The existing working breweries of Castelain, De Clerck, Bécu and Bernoville are examples. Modernisation became the key; new techniques and technologies were expensive, so amalgamations – *Unions* or *Co-opératives* – became common. The Enfants de Gayant brewery, still functioning today as Les Brasseurs de Gayant, was the result of the fusion in 1919 of the activities of four pre-war breweries, three of them already in Douai, the other from a nearby village. Some firms gave up brewing and became merely distributors for other companies. All in all, somewhere in the region of a thousand breweries – half the pre-war total – gave up the ghost within a decade.

The Second World War resulted in further appalling damage and destruction. The only way forward, it seemed was more amalgamation and modernisation. A ruthless market logic imposed itself; ever larger breweries, incorporating expensive equipment, increased production.

The overall consumption of beer declined dramatically for a time, after the war. During the war, in occupied France, wine of reasonable quality was available, if you were lucky enough to get the required ration coupons. Brewers, deprived of good quality ingredients, produced ever poorer and weaker beer. *La petite bière* as it was known, was on average 0.5% ABV. Pierre-André Dubois, retired master-brewer, former president of Les Amis de la Biere and formidable historian of brewing and beer in Northern France, describes the war-time beverage as "fizzy water with a faint taste of hops". Remy Ricour, at St-Sylvestre, remembers the bottle beer, at 0.8% being "reasonable", but the beer in barrels resembling "pisse d'âne" (âne being a donkey). The reputation of beer suffered, that of wine was enhanced. Mineral water, soda water and lemonade became more popular.

The larger brewers, now mainly given to lager-brewing, fought ferociously for their share of a dwindling market; smaller breweries and many of the inter-war *Unions* were taken over or driven into bankruptcy. Competition became even more intense when giant industrial firms from outside the region – and outside the country – started to move in, with huge finances and marketing muscle.

Michael Jackson's World Guide to Beer, first published in 1977, included in his brief chapter on France a devastating chart which demonstrated how "the small brewers were swallowed by the Big Six … in just one decade". The Big Six, in 1977, were BSN Bières, Union des Brasseries, Albra (Heineken), Pelforth, Motte-Cordonnier (Artois) and the Brasseries du Pêcheur who, between them, had swallowed up almost fifty not-especially "small"

Unions, Co-opératives and independent breweries in just ten years.

The Big Six are now the Big Three – BSN/Danone/Kronenbourg, Heineken, and Inter-Brew. They control, at a very conservative estimate, 90% of the market. BSN, a vast industrial conglomerate, has its headquarters in Strasbourg and its two gigantic breweries are at Champigneulles, in Lorraine and Rennes, in Brittany. Interbrew, a Belgian company, has closed down every French brewery it has bought, with the exception of the old Motte-Cordonnier plant, in Armentieres, which no longer brews, but is used as a storage and distribution depot for Interbrew's range of Belgian beers. Heineken, from the Netherlands, bought and modernised the former Pelforth Brewery at Mons-en-Baroeul, near Lille, and still produce a selection of the old Pelforth repertoire from there. Very recently Heineken took a controlling interest in the St Omer Brewery, but have promised to keep brewing to the old portfolio for a minimum of three years.

Driving through Northern France today and looking at seemingly endless bar and cafe signs for Kronenbourg/Kanterbrau, Stella Artois (Interbrew) and Heineken/Pelforth, you might be forgiven for thinking that there are very few beers on offer, none of them, apart from Pelforth, come from the region – and most if not all of them you could sample quite easily without ever leaving Britain.

The secret of survival, for those twenty or truly regional breweries, sharing a tiny fraction of the market, lies in the beer – and it is a remarkable story.

BEER: TRANSLATIONS, EXPLANATIONS AND SOME RECENT HISTORY

Whether a beer is a *bière de soif* or a *bière de dégustation* is largely a matter of personal taste. If you are reading this book, you are almost certainly an *amateur de la bière* – *amateur* in this sense does not mean you are a non-professional, but signifies a beer enthusiast, or a beer lover, someone who is always open to new experiences, tastes and styles, someone who prefers *une bière de dégustation* to a *biere de soif* every time. Congratulations.

The most interesting beers in Northern France are the *bières spéciales* or *bières de specialité*. The first term is precise. A *bière spéciale* is strong – more than 5.5% ABV – and it comes at the top of a league table of officially recognised strengths which begins with a *bière sans alcool* and works its way up through a *bière de table, bière bock* and *bière de luxe*.

A *bière de spécialité* is a beer with a strongly pronounced character – it will almost certainly be a *bière spéciale* as well.

We have to delve into history, ancient and modern, to understand the terms *bière de mars* and *bière de Noël*. Before the days of modern technology, especially of refrigeration and temperature control, the brewing of beer was strictly regulated by the seasons and harvests.

The barley harvest traditionally began on St Arnould's day (19 July) and ended on St Lawrence's day (15 August) – then began the long process of steeping, germination and drying which eventually produced malts. The end of the hop harvest was St Michael's day (29 September). There was a saying "Houblon ne reste pas au ciel après la Saint-Michel" – "hops don't stay in the sky after St Michael's day". After harvesting, hops too required a period of careful drying and preparation.

The brewing year began on 1 October. By using a mix of malts and hops from the previous season, together with some of the new stocks, it was possible to brew an ordinary beer, often called a *bière de débit*, relatively quickly. The first classy beer of the season, however, was the *bière de Noël*, made when the malts and hops of the season were at their very best.

Even better was to come. Beer brewed just before Christmas could be made not just with excellent materials, but would benefit from the Blessings of God over Christmas and, more importantly, from a prolonged period of maturation and very slow secondary fermentation at low temperatures in cold weather – a period *de garde*.

The long-awaited *bière de mars*, universally acclaimed the best beer of the year, was thus a *bière de garde*. Similarly, the best beer brewed in March, then given a long rest in cold cellars, was a *bière de garde*, supplies of which would last through the summer. The best beers thus depended on naturally cold periods of the year.

It was difficult, if not impossible, in those far-off days, to brew in the summer months, mainly because of the dangers of contamination from wild yeasts in the air. There was an old saying "En hiver, brasse qui veut, en été, brasse qui peut" ("In winter, brew when you want, in summer brew when you can" – would be a rough translation). At one time, it was actually forbidden by law to brew between St George's day (23 April) and St Michael's day.

All very well, I hear you saying, but what has all that to do with the modern world? Very little, would be the answer – modern conservation and brewing technologies have rendered much of the old wisdom irrelevant. Powerful national and international malting companies can ship in barley from all over the world – not just Europe – and ensure supplies throughout the year. Large hop dealers can look to markets as far away as the United States and China – again, local seasons are rendered irrelevant.

Parts of the seasonal, regional, tradition remained, though, in Northern France, and many small breweries would make special beers, from local ingredients, especially for their best private customers, for Christmas. By the mid-1970s though, the tradition, and the breweries, had all but disappeared.

There was one extraordinary exception – the Brasserie Duyck, at Jenlain, near Valenciennes was still making a strong *ambrée, a bière de garde* utilising comparatively modern techniques, old ideas. As far as anyone can remember, the beer had a long history, going back to the 1930s – when it eventually acquired a label, the label said *la bière de garde de la Brasserie Duyck à Jenlain*. The brewery brochures today talk about a beer originally brewed for agricultural workers in the springtime, so maybe it was a *bière de mars*.

In 1968, the name was shortened to simply "Jenlain". In the 1970s, students at the Catholic University in Lille discovered it on sale at a local grocer's hop – and it became more and more popular. Jenlain was nicely presented, in a 75cl bottle, corked and wired like champagne. (Legend has it that this particular tradition began during the immediate post-war years, when shortages of glass led Monsieur Duyck to collect old champagne and cider bottles from Jenlain and surrounding villages to supplement his supplies. The counter-theory says that this presentation was traditional and had been used for generations for valued customers). Most important of all, as far as the students were concerned, Jenlain was powerful, tasty and cheap – Monsieur Duyck had kept quality up, his prices down.

One by one, a handful of other small breweries changed tack, stopped trying to compete with the giant industrial brewers, and gambled on a special beer, often rediscovered from an old family recipe book. Some of them acknowledge the influence of the pioneering Jenlain – others claim to have made the decision alone. The change often occurred when there was a generation change at the brewery. The terms *bière de garde, brassée à l'ancienne* (brewered by the old method) and *brasserie artisinale* (cottage industry production) began to be used and displayed more and more prominently. Brand-new micro breweries used the same vocabulary.

Bière de garde need further explanation. It

does *not* mean a beer which can be kept indefinitely, like a fine wine, to mature with age. Most *bières de garde* are ready for drinking immediately; after a year or so, they will start to deteriorate. The exception to the rule is the beer which is re-fermented in the bottle – a *bière sur lie*, or *bière sur levure*. Provided they are kept upright, in cool conditions and away from light, such beers may perform interestingly in future years. A *bière sur lie* may be naturally cloudy – *trouble* – there may be a warning on the bottle to that effect.

There are no official regulations about a *bière de garde* and I am not sure that it can be called a beer "style", although it is often so described. It is assumed that they are all initially top-fermented, as was the tradition in Northern France – today, many of the famous ones are not. The periods of *garde* vary – from two to twelve weeks. A *bière de garde* can be *blonde* (pale), *ambrée* (amber, or more likely, copper-coloured), *brune* (brown) or very occasionally *rousse* – russet, or reddish-brown – somewhere between *ambrée* and *brune*), according to the malts used. It is available all the year round. (A *bière blanche*, or white beer, is a different animal altogether – it is a wheat beer, and may be *trouble*).

The notion of a *bière de mars* was redeveloped quite recently in the region, by the Ricour brewery at St-Sylvestre, in French Flanders. They did a test brew, of 80 hectolitres, of a top-fermented *ambrée*, made from carefully selected malts, hopped with Brewers' Gold and Hallertau, given a prolonged period of *garde* and coming out at 7% ABV – far stronger than anything else the brewery was making at the time. The new beer was test-flown by taking a stand at various agricultural shows in the region and asking for a reaction from customers. The reaction was ecstatic and production began in earnest in 1984.

In 1990, encouraged perhaps by other breweries which were doing the same sort of thing, *Les Brasseurs de France* threw its considerable marketing weight behind a national campaign to launch *les bières de mars*. A Good Thing, of course – nowadays the arrival of the *bières de mars* is greeted by a publicity blitz in most of the bars in the country.

Les Brasseurs drew up guidelines for the new beers – *une charte-produit* – which stated that a *bière de mars* should be *légérement ambrée*, thanks to a judicious mix of pale and aromatic malts, that it should be "fresh and aromatic", with a strength of 4.5 to 5% ABV – and that it should only be on sale during the month of March. The large regional breweries and the national behemoths signed up immediately, having recently rediscovered the value of tradition.

The smaller breweries stayed away, reluctant to be constrained by rules about strength, colour and availability – but continued to produce their spring beers. St-Sylvestre's *bière de mars* was renamed *Bière Nouvelle*. The smaller brewers' spring beers remain, by and large, more interesting than the officially recognised ones. Try, besides the St-Sylvestre *Bière Nouvelle*, the Cuvée de Jonquilles of the Brasserie Bailleux and the *bières de mars* of La Choulette and Castelain.

Often, the key recipe which rescued a small brewery was an old Christmas favourite, never previously given a name, but made for special clients every year, now dug out of the archive, given a new name and sold all the year round. Opinions differ as to which brewery started to market a specially names *bière de Noël* – the Brasserie Jeanne D'Arc claims they were the first to launch the "new" concept, in 1975. Other retired brewers I have spoken to say they were doing this for years beforehand, without the marketing clout and skill. The Brasserie Terken have been producing their *Christmas ambrée*, for their own private customers, since 1948.

Everyone has taken up the idea now. In 1986, *Les Amis de la Bière*, together with the Syndicat des Brasseurs du Nord de La France, began their annual presentation of Christmas beers. They have drawn up some criteria – a *bière de Noël* should be strong, aromatic, coloured within a spectrum *ambrée-brune*, with malt pronounced over hop, specially presented (Christmas label, usually 75cl special bottle), *haut de gamme* (top of the range), sold between 15 November and the end of the year. Most breweries, large and small, were prepared to sign up to these loose rules and the Christmas campaign is enthusiastic and popular.

The *bières de Noël* are invariably good, but difficult, if not impossible to qualify or analyse, year in year out. Some breweries simply relabel existing *ambrée* or *brune* brews, many change their Christmas recipes slightly from year to year. And of course, you have to be in France sometime between mid-November and the end of December to get at them at all, since none of the beers are exported.

The Christmas period is, notwithstanding all that, a good time to visit the country and join in the fun. Several breweries have a weekend in early November, of *portes-ouvertes*, which mean they throw open their doors to the general public and invite all-comers to try out the season's *bière de Noël*. There is the famous day, or rather, evening presentation by the *Syndicat* and *Les Amis de la Bière*, in a different town each year – and practically every bar in the region will have a *bière de Noël* on offer, either on draught or in bottle.

Finally, there is one more term to take on board. Several of the *bieres de spécialitées* have an additional blue-and-red-badged label on the bottle, indicating that it is one of *Les Excellences Nord-Pas-de-Calais*. *L'Association des Excellences du Nord-Pas de Calais,* formed in 1991, seeks to promote authentic regional products, such as cheeses, confectionery, honey, chocolates and gin. As far as beers go, their stamp of approval is not quite the equivalent of a wine's *appelation controlée*, but it is only awarded to breweries based in the region and beers which are made from at least 50% regional ingredients (malts and hops) and which are independently tested on a regular basis to ensure that the quality remains constant and high.

Dans la Tradition   DEPUIS 1885   Bière de Garde

THE BREWERIES

Brasserie des Amis-Réunis

2 avenue du Collège
59230 St-Amand-Les-Eaux
Tel: 03.27.48.77.77
Fax: 03.27.48.80.00

St-Amand-Les-Eaux is a spa-town surrounded by forests, on the very edge of the former coal mining belt, north-west of Valenciennes. Until recently, it was best known for the old abbey bell-tower and its charming tinkling *carillon* – and the sale of bottled health-giving spring water.

The brand new Brasserie des Amis-Réunis is in the former abattoir buildings of St-Amand, some way out of town by the canalised River Scarpe, on the Avenue du Collège. Head for the centre of St-Amand (which can get very busy on Friday mornings – market day), signposted from the A23 Valenciennes-Lille motorway. At the very end of the main square, turn right down the Boulevard Louise des Bettignies. As this road crosses the canal, it becomes the Avenue du Collège. The brewery is on the right, part of a small, still-developing industrial estate.

The Brasserie des Amis-Réunis, opened in late 1997, has several claims to fame, not the least of which is that it was part financed by L'Association Germinal, an organisation formed by the film director, Claude Berri and regional and local authorities. Co-directors of L'Association include the stars of the recent Berri movie version of Germinal – Gérard Dépardieu, Miou-Miou and the folk-singer/actor Renaud – all household names in France. You don't get many breweries with such glamorous backing.

Emile Zola's brilliant and shattering novel deals with the appalling suffering experienced by miners in the Valenciennois in the latter part of the nineteenth century; a hundred years on, the making of the film coincided almost exactly with the final agonies and closures of pits and the end of mining in the North of France, with devastating consequences for the economy of the region. Berri wanted to put money from the film into schemes to provide employment. After several false starts, the brewery in St-Amand looks like being the first success story of the enterprise – although there were raised eyebrows in some quarters at the choice of a spa town which has never had anything to do with mining. Earlier choices for the site of a brewery disappeared into the labyrinthine complexities and rivalries of local politics.

Olivier Forest, who runs the new brewery, was the owner of Brasserie Steinbeer, at Évin-Malmaison, just outside Douai, from 1984 to 1994, before selling out to an English run company. (The latter then gambled heavily and disastrously on cheap lagers for the Calais cash-and-carry-it-home-in-a-battered-white-Transit-van English market. They went bust and it is difficult not to gloat).

While at Évin-Malmaison, Forest had developed an intriguing and much admired top-fermented *bière sur lie* called *L'Ecume des Jours* (7% ABV), sold mainly in the traditional corked and wired champagne-style bottle. When he left, he took the label with him, and continued to brew the beer in exile at the Brasserie Brunehaut, just over the border in Belgium. L'Ecume des Jours has now returned to France, and is part of the current repertoire of the Brasserie des Amis-Réunis.

The year before the new brewery finally opened, while torturous negotiations were still under way, Monsieur Forest introduced another beer, brewed at Brunehaut, but optimistically named *L'Abbatiale de St-Amand*. It was again top-fermented, again *sur lie*, at 7% ABV and sold primarily in the large corked bottles. This creation, however, was spiced up with juniper berries – *baies de Genièvriers*. This combination was not as unusual as it may sound. It had long been the habit of hardened French beer drinkers in the North to jazz up a *demi* with a shot of gin, or *genièvre*. L'Abbatiale was launched in a pre-emptive strike of great verve and there were close-up photographs of the bottle, with the still developing site in the background, in the local and national press. Local grocers stocked up and sold well.

The latest beer, introduced when the Brasserie des Amis-Réunis finally opened, could be the most successful of the lot – not because it is necessarily the best, but because of the name, *Germinal*. The book is well known in France, the Berri's film did well at the domestic box-office – Germinal is a tremendous, instantly recognised brand name. The film world connection could be even more important; there is talk of Germinal being sold in the world wide much-hyped Planet Hollywood bar/restaurants. The beer is top-fermented, very lightly hopped – and this time filtered and sold in 33cl crown-capped bottles. Strength is 6.5% ABV. The bottle carries a label with a cockerel crowing over pit-head gear, with the slogan "La Bière des moments forts" – "for life's most intense moments". Not quite sure what to make of that. All the company's beers are spiced, Belgian fashion.

If the brewery does establish itself within the French and European market (let alone exploit the Planet Hollywood possibilities), everyone will benefit, because Olivier Forest is obliged by the terms of the agreement with L'Association Germinal to plough 5% of his profits from the sales of Germinal back into the organisation and the money will then be used to finance other job enhancing projects in the old mining region.

Within months of the opening of the brewery, Olivier Forest, who has an eye for detail and a commercial opportunity, produced *La Bière du Chamane de la Grande Braderie de Lille*. The Braderie is the biggest second-hand goods fair in France, held in Lille during the first weekend in September – much more of this later, in the Gazeteer Section. *Moules-frites* (mussels and chips) is the staple dish of the Braderie and the Chamane is a recently invented (c1996) traditional figure who strides around the proceedings in a costume of mussel shells, holding a chip-fork trident. (I am not making any of this up). By November 1997, the brewery had produced a *Germinal ambrée* top-fermented, at 6.5% ABV.

These are early days at the Brasserie des Amis-Réunis – production capacity is about 9000 hectolitres a year, but that could soon be increased to 15000 hectolitres. There are plans for a restaurant next door, with windows looking out into the mysteries of the brewery. The local authorities of St-Amand are also extremely keen on another idea – a shop selling regional produce and ready-cooked meals. At the moment, the only other business up and running on the abattoir site is a meat packing plant.

It should be possible to buy beers at the brewery. There may be tours. Best to contact Olivier Forest to find out the current state of play.

Brasserie d'Annoeullin
4, Grand'Place
59112 Annoeullin
Tel: 03.20.86.88.60
Fax: 03.20.86.69.27

Annoeullin is not the sort of place which normally figures in guidebooks; it is a nondescript largish agricultural village of sooty red-brick, midway between Lille and Lens, but off even the lesser roads which join those two towns. (It is technically in the *arrondissement* of Lille). The Grand'Place, otherwise known as the Place General De Gaulle, is a tiny triangular car park directly in front of the Hotel de Ville. Park here, if you can, and the secretive alleyway leading to the Brasserie d'Anoeullin is directly opposite. There is a new, rather fine sign, hanging from a wrought-iron frame in the wall – unfortunately, the sign is one-end towards you and thus almost invisible as you look from the Town Hall. You have enough clues now to find the place.

The brewery was founded in 1905, by a farmer-brewer called Auguste Maille. It survived the First World War, although the Germans had turned it into a fortified strong-point; it was only ten kilometres from their front line. You will pass signs to a German military cemetery if you come here via the neighbouring village of Carvin. Monsieur Maille had to chip away the concrete to get his brewery back. Three generations later, his great grand-daughter married Bernard Lepers, who was himself a descendant of a family of brewers, hop-merchants and maltsters. Their son, Bertrand Lepers, who now runs the brewery, with his wife Yolande, can thus claim to be a fifth generation brewer, from both sides of the family, a formidable pedigree.

The latest generation masterminded the brewery's survival. Bertrand can remember the time, not more than twenty years ago, when their main customers were schools, who required beers of feeble strength for their pupils, and private clients, who took delivery of beers each week. There was a slightly more interesting Christmas beer, specially brewed for the best customers. From about 1975 onwards, this was brewed and sold all the year round as a top-fermented *bière de specialité*, called **Pastor Ale** (6.5% ABV). Gradually, Pastor Ale became the major production. Bertrand, who has a wicked sense of humour beneath a placid exterior, advertised it by claiming "C'est une symphonie" – Pastorale Symphony?

In 1985, after a search through the old Brasserie Maille recipe books, he came across another interesting beer, a *bière de froment*, made with 30% wheat. (It just so happened that old farmer Maille had a surplus of wheat in the year the beer was first brewed). With some readjustment, the old beer became a new one, called **L'Angelus**. It was a success from the very beginning, and soon overtook Pastor Ale in popularity and sales and is now mainstay of the brewery.

L'Angelus, pale gold, lemony, faintly spicy, is a champagne of beers and without doubt, a classic. In France, it appears in fancy restaurants such as the L'Huitrière in Lille and Le Flavio in Le Touquet and there is a significant export market to Germany, Italy and the USA. The label has a reproduction of the famous painting by Jean-François Millet of the pious peasants at prayer in the fields; on the other hand, the poster campaign for the beer at one time had a photograph of a stunning blonde arm-wrestling a man with a caption which read "Une blonde qui cache bien son jeu". Since L'Angelus is a whopping 7% ABV, the poster is a more accurate summation of the beer's properties. Most production is bottled – there is some draught, but it is difficult to find. One outlet is the Vole Hole, in Boulogne.

L'Angelus is re-tuned, with the help of caramel malts, into an amber *Bière de Mars*, at 5.5% ABV, while the darker L'Angelus de Noël is back to 7.5%.

The brewery at Annoeullin is something of a classic in itself, in a cramped rickety building with ancient looking machinery. The fermentation tanks are stored in between old cattle byres – a reminder of the brewery's agricultural past. It's a shame that the Lepers cannot, in the normal run of things, cope with visitors, although one can quite understand why – there is only a tiny workforce and they are all too busy producing 4000 hectolitres of beer a year to show people round. From time to time, they do manage an open day – *portes ouvertes* – but they are few and far between and usually just for local residents and those in the know.

You can get as far as the office, up a flight of wooden stairs on the right of the alleyway, and buy beers at the brewery, but only in cases of a dozen bottles at a time. Try the shop, Aux Caves d'Annoeullin, also in the Grand'Place, for smaller samples – and for a good selection of the better beers from other breweries in Northern France.

Brasserie Bailleux

(Café-Restaurant Au Baron)
Place au Fond des Rocs
59570 Gussignies
Tel: 03.27.66.88.61
Fax: 03.27.39.89.04

You will need a good map to find the Brasserie Bailleux. From the N49 at Bavay, take the D24 to and though Bellignies. At the wayside cross on the right, turn left for Gussignies. Follow the small signs for *Brasserie Artisinale* and/or *Au Baron*. Eventually, there is a steep, curving descent to the stream called L'Hogneau. Park at the Fond des Rocs, by the stream. The brewery/restaurant is the tall modern red-brick building behind shrubs and trees over the bridge on the other side of the water.

Back in 1973, Alain Bailleux took over a small café at Fond des Rocs. It was already a secretive, but popular rural weekend retreat for Belgian and French visitors – by 1986 it had become so popular that the café was rebuilt and extended to accommodate 60 diners in a restaurant. Three years later, the micro-brewery was added and Alain Bailleux had exactly what he had wanted all along – a restaurant with its own beer supply – something he had seen years before in Germany. Bailleux comes from a family of brewery engineers, so he knew exactly what he was doing.

The brewery came on stream on the 8th of June, which is Saint Médard's Day in the French calendar; the first beer, an *ambrée*, was called **Saison St-Médard**. The term "saison" is a gesture towards the style of beer of that name, well-known just across the border in Belgium. In the same year, 1989, at Christmas, the **Saison-St-Médard, Cuvée de Noël** appeared. This is a *brune* – in effect, the Saison with torrified malts added. (It has also appeared, briefly, under the label Cuvée des Marbriers, this latter a tribute to the marble workers who used to work in the quarries around the villages of Bellignies).

The Hogneau is a pleasant little river, bubbling away between steep wooded banks. In springtime it is gloriously illuminated by bankside daffodils – *jonquilles*. In 1990, Alain Bailleux was inspired to produce his **Cuvée des Jonquilles**, his version of a *bière de mars*. Like all his beers, this is top-fermented, hopped with Brewers' Gold and Hallertau, given a long period of *garde* and re-fermented in the bottle. All three are 7% ABV.

There has been little publicity, no thrusting marketing, just honest-to-goodness hard work in this quiet little corner of the world, so it is pleasing to note that the Bailleux beers are rated very highly by experts in France and elsewhere. The Cuvée des Jonquilles, especially, is acknowledged as one of the finest beers of the French revival.

Although two out of the three beers are seasonal, they are usually available all the year round.

Go round to the back of the café/restaurant, during brewery opening hours, climb the steps and order your beers. You are in the middle of the action – the tiny staff will be busy brewing, bottling and labelling. You don't really need a "tour"; if your French is up to it, someone will explain to you what's going on. Production is 800 hectolitres a year.

Ideally, you should plan your visit to include a meal. Au Baron is run by Alain Bailleux' son and his wife – the menu is regional, seasonal, memorable, and features some spectacular work at the grill, which is a log fire inside an old brewery copper. The place is usually full of Belgians, who know their stuff, and trek down the narrow lanes on pilgrimage to France.

The brewery is open 0800 – 1200, 1400 – 1700, every day except Wednesday. The café/restaurant opens only Friday (from 1500), Saturday and Sunday (from 1100). In the high season, there may be extra days – best to telephone ahead to check. Best to book, no matter when you go.

Ferme-Brasserie Beck

Eeckelstraete
59270 Bailleul
Tel: 03.28.49.03.90
Fax: 03.28.42.28.32

Bailleul is just off the A25 Dunkirk-Lille Autoroute, west of Armentieres. From Bailleul's Grand'Place, take the D25 Rue d'Ypres, but after only 150 metres, turn right – the road is signposted to the military and civilian cemeteries and there should also be the first of several small signs for "Gîte-Ferme Beck, Bière Hommelpap". Once past the cemeteries, the road peters out into a pot-holed country lane. Follow the Beck signs, past several farms, up into the hills. You will know you have arrived when you see the hop-posts and wires in the fields around you.

Denys Beck is a farmer who you would think had his hands full with his cattle, poultry, mixed cereal crops and hops, plus a gîte, which provides accommodation, usually for school parties who arrive to spend a short educational holiday on the farm and in the surrounding countryside. He is also the president of the local hop-growers' co-operative. A few years ago, his mind turned to the possibility of brewing beer. "Without beer", says Monsieur Beck, "Flanders would lose its character. And without hops, there would be no beer. It seemed a logical step".

In 1994, Yves Castelain, of Brasseries Castelain fame, bought out a defunct micro-brewery in the Auvergne and sold the equipment on to Denys Beck. The "new" micro is now up and running in a new wooden building, brightly painted with dancing, boozing country folk, in front of the old farmhouse. If there is no-one about in the brewery, go round to the yard at the back and knock on the farmhouse door. You may have to persevere, for it is quite possible that Denys, his wife Christiane and everyone else, will be at work in the gîte or in the fields nearby.

There is only one beer and it is called *Hommelpap*, a Flemish word which denotes the celebrations at hop-harvest-time. Hommelpap, described as an *ambrée*, is copper-coloured, with a dense head – it is top-fermented and the hops used are Target and Magnum for bitterness, Hallertau and Strisselspalt for aroma. I suspect variations, because I am pretty sure that Monsieur Beck experiments from time to time – he is a hop grower after all. The label on the bottle is hop-cone styled and shaped and announces "brassé en Flandre par le Houblonnier" – "brewed in Flanders by the hop-grower".

Hommelpap is filtered but not pasteurised, and comes in the now-traditional 75cl corked and wired bottle. ABV is 7%. Production is very limited – somewhere in the region of 150 hectolitres each year. The Becks advise that their beer should be drunk within a couple of months.

The beer does not seem to be available anywhere in Bailleul except the Tourist Office, who usually have cartons of three bottles, or two bottles and a badged glass, for sale. Wherever you buy it, it is quite expensive, compared with other *bières artisinales*.

During the tourist season, you can tour the hop fields and brewery, ending up with a tasting of Hommelpap and a bite to eat – *L'Assiette du Brasseur*. Bookings are done through the Tourist Office and there is a small fee. On special occasions, Denys Beck picks up the party in Bailleul and ferries them to the farm in a horse-drawn wagon. He reckons the best time to visit is in June, when he swears the hop-bines grow up to 7 centimetres in a single day. In August and late September/early October, just before and just after the harvest, there are special trips around this and other hop fields.

Brasserie Bécu

10, rue Verlaine
62118 Fampoux
Tel: 03.21.55.97.57
Fax: 03.21.48.24.52

Fampoux is a small village a few kilometres east of Arras. Coming from Arras, follow the D42 via Athies. From the A1 Autoroute, come off at the N50 and follow the signs south from Gavrelle. Fampoux is built on a hillside, the huge brick church is at the top, the brewery at the bottom, near the wooded valley of the River Scarpe. Park in the cobbled brewery yard.

The whole of Fampoux is built of 1920s red brick; the village was on the front line during the First World War and was all but obliterated. If you arrive via the quiet country lane from the main Arras-Douai Road, you will pass several tiny British battlefield cemeteries. The neighbouring village of Roeux, a kilometre away, has just unearthed and published the memoirs of a German officer, called *Dans les tranchée devant Arras.*

Henri-Joseph Bécu founded the brewery in 1862. By 1918, all that remained under a heap of rubble was the shaft of the 60 metre well which supplied water up through the deep chalk beds. The brewery was rebuilt – spectacularly rebuilt – in 1925, with compensation money, *dommages de guerre*. It is an impressive complex of buildings, an architectural historian's delight, with the massive brewery itself, a wing given over to malting, a dovecote and a handsome master-brewer's house, all in highly decorated brick with stone rustication and fancy wood and wrought-iron work crawling all over the place. The reverse swastikas decorating the building are nothing to do with the SS, but are ancient Egyptian signs for prosperity. The whole estate is surrounded by a high brick wall and entered via huge ornamental gates.

The state-of-the-art brewery of the 1920s crumbled in the very different economic climate of the 1960s and was closed in 1963, although, crucially, the family kept control of the land and buildings. Enter the brothers Pierre and Henri Bécu, the sixth generation of the family, who decided to re-open for business, in a comparatively modest way, after a thirty year gap. Paul, with his wife Anne, began to experiment with a new range of beers in 1992 and, by 1994, they were up and running with a micro-brewery almost hidden away in one corner of the old maltings.

Their regular beers, a *blonde*, an *ambrée* and a *brune* are all called **L'Atrébate**. The Atrabates were the Gaulish tribe who controlled the region of Artois when Caesar and his Latin tribe arrived. L'Atrébate(s) are all made from malts from locally grown barley and hops from Flanders. Monsieur Bécu is curiously reticent about the hop varieties, claiming that the malts are far more important. High-alpha hops are added, he says, in minute quantities, like "salt and pepper to a steak". The yeast is a secret too, although the beers are certainly top fermented. There are three fermentations, five days at 22° C, three to four weeks at 2-5° C, and in bottle or barrel for a further two weeks at 24° C. All three beers emerge at 6% ABV.

They are neither filtered nor pasteurised and when poured from the usual type of 75cl bottle, tend to behave spectacularly. They certainly have to be poured carefully because of the thick lees and riotous head. Monsieur Bécu says he has modelled his best-selling *blonde* on Duvel. When L'Atrébate is on form, this is not so far-fetched as it sounds. The problem would seem to be that of achieving consistency.

There are seasonal offerings as well – L'Atrébate *Spéciale Noël*, dark, luscious and strong, at 8%ABV, while L'Atrébate *Spéciale Mars* comes back to the standard 6%. This latter also appears as Saint-Elixir for the three day *Fête des Rats* at nearby Arras in May. Total production is 1000 hectolitres per year.

It would be fascinating to tour the whole brewery – Pierre Bécu thinks so too, but in the first place, he's too busy and secondly, there would be problems with the French equivalent of the Health and Safety Executive. One day, he hopes the money will be found to turn the whole place into a working museum. In the meantime, you have to content yourself with a look around the main buying and tasting room, which is filled with ancient, rusted, cobwebbed machinery, with tattered drive-belts from an old steam engine, disappearing mysteriously into the ceiling. For a small charge, you can see a short video of the brewing process, made by Monsieur Bécu himself. Better, really, to spend the money on another bottle of L'Atrébate.

A draught version of L'Atrébate is usually available at the Estaminet des Arcades, in the Place des Héros, Arras.

The Brasserie Bécu is open Monday to Friday 0800 – 1200 and 1400 – 1800. It is always best to telephone ahead.

A few yards from the Brasserie Bécu, in the same street, the Rue Verlaine, there is a sign on a high blank wall announcing the sale of cider and apple juice. Go through the nearby gate and you will find yourself in a huge, pungent, farmyard. Christian Daulle runs a mixed farm and, a decade ago, with the encouragement of his brother Hubert, added cider to the repertoire. The apples come from Normandy, Brittany and the Thiérache, but Christian has now planted an orchard of his own locally and is waiting patiently for the trees to mature. The first press which the brothers Daulle acquired was a wonderful old wooden museum piece – it has been replaced by an ultra-modern affair from Switzerland.

The ciders, a *brut* and a *demi-sec* are matured for two months, then filtered, but not pasteurised. Both are 4.5% ABV, and sold in 75cl bottles, corked and wired like the *bières de garde* in this part of France.

Ferme Daulle, 4 rue Paul Verlaine, 62118 Fampoux. Tel: 03.21.55.50.56. Open every day – Sundays "might be a problem".

Brasserie de Bernoville

34, rue de Martimprey
02110 Aisonville
Tel: 03.23.66.00.40

The scattered village of Aisonville-Bernoville is well off the beaten track, deep in silent countryside on the D960 between Bohain-en-Vermandois and Guise, in the *département* of Aisne. When you reach Aisonville, turn off the main road, following the signs for Montigny, then left again past the Post Office, again following Montigny/St-Quentin. The brewery, which is actually in Bernoville, is a large handsome building of rusticated cream stone, but stands well back on the right from the road, behind gravel driveways and patches of rough green grass. There is a cardboard sign slung from a lamp post by the road, which says *Brasserie Artisinale*. Drive into the brewery yard and if no-one is about, ring the bell, either on the wall of the low building to the right, or at the top of the stairs leading to the farmhouse on the left.

The original brewery was built here in 1850 and lasted until 1918, when it was razed to the ground by the retreating German Army. (The Canal de St Quentin, some kilometres to the west, was part of the formidable defences which the Germans called the Siegfried Line and the Allies the Hindenburg Line. The line was breached in September 1918 and the war ended a few weeks later).

The Brasserie Montfourney, as it was then called, was rebuilt in 1920 and fitted out with steam-powered second-hand Belgian machinery from Tournai, with the help of reparations money. It finally gave up the ghost and closed down in the 1960s. Thirty-odd years later, the buildings and land were bought by a farmer, Philippe Depierre, whose own property is near Bellenglise, practically on top of the old Siegfried Line. Monsieur Depierre installed a micro-brewery, largely comprising old dairy equipment, in a few room of the vast rambling old buildings at Bernoville and began brewing in 1994. (There was some brewing tradition, way back in the Depierre family line – his great grandfather had been a farmer-brewer, but had given up after the First World War).

In 1997, he bought a complete set of brewery equipment from a defunct German brewery in the Black Forest and transported it back to Bernoville. By the time you read this, everything should be installed and working and production will have been upped from 200 hectolitres to 600 hectolitres or more each year. Jerry Goret, a cheerful Belgian brewer, who used to work at a brewery in Mons until Interbrew bought it out and closed it down, is in charge of production.

There are two regular beers at the moment, both of them top-fermented, given a period of *garde* and refermented in the bottle. The labels proudly announce *Brassée a l'Ancienne* and *Fabrication Artisinale*. **La Bernoville** (7% ABV) is an *ambrée* made from French and Belgian malts and Saaz and Hallertau hops, while **La Bière du Pays de Guise** (5.5%), made with pale malt and the same hops, is a *bière blonde*. The Christmas beer is the *ambrée*, upped to 8% ABV. They are sold mainly in 75cl or 25cl bottles, both crown-capped, although there is some in 30 and 50 litre *fûts*, or steel barrels. The Bernoville beers are little known, even in Northern France, but they are all delicious and deserve much wider distribution.

You can tour the brewery, if you are part of a group of at least 15 people, you make an appointment by telephone several weeks ahead, and you are prepared to pay 15F a head, which includes a tasting of the Bernoville beers. That all sounds a bit complicated, but it would be well worth the effort, because it really is a fascinating place. The main building and maltings have much of that 1920s Belgian equipment still silently in place (although some of it may now have been moved to make room for the "new" German acquisitions).

The cellars provide the strangest experience of all – they survived the German destruction of 1918 and are thus untouched since 1850. There are the remains of the boiler, and a startlingly sophisticated series of low, brick built tunnels with tiny sets of rails running through them, leading to hoists. The barrels, it would appear, were trundled around the cellars on bogies, and hoisted up to daylight via the lift shafts.

There can't be many places in Europe where you can see substantial parts of a nineteenth century French brewery, a Belgian reconstruction of the 1920s, and an imported German brewery of the 1970s, all on the same site – and then taste and buy some splendid samples of "new" but old-style French country beers.

Brasserie Artisinale du Cambier

18 bis rue Pastuer
59265 Aubigny-au-Bac
Tel: 03.27.92.09.95

Aubigny-au-Bac is on the N43, between Douai and Cambrai. "Bac" means a ferry, but there has not been a ferry at Aubigny for some three hundred years. Centuries ago, the valley of the River Sensée used to flood regularly and boats were needed – now the N43 dips and climbs briefly and you might not even notice the river at all. Coming from Douai, from the north, take the first road signposted on the left to Aubigny. This is the Rue Pasteur – the tiny Brasserie Artisinale du Cambier, a new one-storey building of red brick, with red-tiled roof and brown shutters, stands back from the road almost immediately on the left. It looks more like a large garage than a brewery and the only clue is a small notice on the free standing letter box at the beginning of the tarmac drive.

Gérard Caudrelier's brewing pedigree is impressive. His father and grandfather before him were brewers. He was trained at Nancy, Roubaix and Douai and worked in several breweries, latterly the Brasseurs de Gayant, in Douai. In 1982, he broke away to independence and set up the Brasserie Caudrelier on a farm at Fressain, a small village northwest of Aubigny-au-Bac. It proved to be an over-ambitious exercise, and was discontinued in 1989.

The new brewery, launched in 1997, is much smaller – each brewing session produces 6 hectolitres instead of the 60 he was turning out at Fressain. There is just one beer, which in fact is the same one he produced at the original brewery; it is called *Iris Beer*, a very odd name. Iris turns out to be the name of a much-loved but long-defunct horse Monsieur Caudrelier once owned. I never did find out which his beer is a beer and not a *bière*.

Iris Beer, an *ambrée*, is made from pale and caramel malts, with Strisselspalt and Tettnang hops, plus a mystery item – a "very old" hop, says Monsieur Caudrelier, "called Bourgogne". He would not be drawn to any further explanation – one can only assume that the hope is in pelleted form and has been around a long time. The beer is top-fermented for a week, then allowed to mature for a month, before being re-fermented in the bottle.

At the moment, Iris beer is sold exclusively in 75cl corked and wired bottles. Money is tight, so Monsieur Caudrelier is supplementing his limited supply of bought-in bottles with old champagne and cider bottles. History coming full circle – this is exactly what Raymond Duyck is said to have done in the early pioneering days of Jenlain.

Iris beer, Monsieur Caudrelier hopes, will soon be for sale in local shops, and perhaps at the roadside stalls along the N43 close to Aubigny-au-Bac, which sell local produce, mainly long tresses of the smoked garlic from nearby Arleux. It may also be available at the Taverne du Ch'Ti in Arras. You can, of course, buy at the brewery – and the place is so small you will be able to "tour" the brewery at the same time. Best to telephone ahead, to make sure someone is at home.

Brasserie Castelain

13, rue Pasteur
Bénifontaine
62410 Wingles
Tel: 03.21.08.68.68
Fax: 03.21.08.68.60

Bénifontaine is a rural village in old coalmining country, north of Lens and just off the N47. Follow the signs for Wingles, then Bénifontaine. You will see the brewery on the left, just before you reach a small roundabout on the outskirts of the village. Negotiate the roundabout, go up the Rue Pasteur and drive in through the brewery gates on the left. There is usually space in the large car park among the workforce's cars and brewery lorries, ancient and modern.

Although this is not at all normal tourist territory, the Brasserie Castelain is extraordinarily welcoming and well organised for visitors. If you want to tour the brewery, ring up beforehand and ask to speak to Fabrice Gaudé. Fabrice speaks English, and likes British tourists, because he reckons they know more about beer, and ask more interesting questions, than the normal run of customers. (He confesses to struggling a bit with Geordie, Scottish and Welsh accents). The tour is comprehensive and fascinating and includes a museum and model hop field as well as all parts of the brewery. You end up in a tempting and well-stocked shop.

Tours by appointment Tuesday to Friday, from 0900 – 1200, 1400 – 1800. Tour without an appointment on Saturday morning 0900 – 1100. There is a charge of 20F per person, which includes a beer

The Brasseries Castelain celebrated, in 1996, "70 ans de passion", by which was meant, among other things, that it was first opened in 1926. The founders were the brothers François, Seyran and Cornil Delomel. Roland Castelain took over the brewery in 1966 and handed it over to his children, Yves and Annick, in the mid-1970s. These were desperate times, with old markets collapsing, industrial conglomerates on the prowl; Yves took a gamble – and the gamble was called Ch'Ti.

For Christmas 1978, harking back to an old tradition, he decided to brew a special beer, stronger than usual, for his best customers. The beer was carefully made, with the very best of ingredients, and allowed to mature for eight weeks – this was Ch'Ti, a blonde *biére de garde*. (Ch'Ti is a Picard dialect term which has come to mean anyone, or anything, from the North). The response was enthusiastic and Yves took the dramatic and courageous decision to drop everything else in the brewery's repertoire and concentrate only on Ch'Ti. The Christmas beer became the all-the-year-round beer in 1979; the label on the bottle depicted a miner's head, complete with helmet and lamp The rest, as they say, is history. The success of Ch'Ti, and the Brasserie Castelain has been quite astonishing.

Ch'Ti Blonde (6.4%ABV) is brewed by infusion with pale malts. The hops are Saaz and Northern Brewers Gold from Flanders. Fermentation uses an ale yeast, but at low temperature. There is a long period (a minimum of six weeks) of secondary fermentation at 0° C – the "garde". The beer is filtered, but not pasteurised. (Ironic, given that the brewery is in the Rue Pasteur). Ch'Ti is available in corked and wired bottles of 75cl and crown-capped bottles of 25cl and on draught in selected bars.

The Castelain range now includes *Ch'Ti Ambrée* (5.4% ABV), *Ch'Ti Brune* (6.4% ABV) and *Ch'Ti Triple* (7.5% ABV). In 1984, *Jade* (4.6% ABV), an organic beer, made from spray-free malts and Bio Perle and Aurora hops was added to the list. The latest beer, launched in 1996, is *La Saint-Patron* (7.5% ABV), a pale *bière sur lie*, which undergoes a third fermentation in the bottle. There are seasonal beers, a *Bière de Mars* and, unusually, two *Cuvées de Nöel*, a *blonde* and an *ambrée* – the *blonde* is the original Christmas beer where it all began, back in 1978.

Production at the brewery has soared. In the 1960s, it was 5,000 hectolitres a year, now it is

30,000 and by the year 2000, Yves Castelain is aiming for 50,000 hectolitres. Ch'Ti, still the jewel in the crown and 60% of total production, is known throughout France and is exported to America and Japan. In Britain, it has penetrated beyond the connoisseur market of specialist shops. The *ambrée* appeared in Sainsbury's, albeit under the supermarket's own label of Bière de Garde – it is now on offer under its own label in Safeways. In the North of France, *Tavernes des Ch'Ti* have started to appear and a kind of satellite station has opened – the Brasserie St Poloise, at Saint Pol-sur-Ternoise, is run by Yves' son, Bertrand.

In spite of all these changes, Yves Castelain clings doggedly to his roots – "Nous preservons toujours l'Authentique" is a much-used slogan in their publicity, but it is much more than just a slogan. The brewery, although immaculate, modern and efficient, is still a folksy kind of place, with a wooden carving of St Arnould in a prominent place, looking over the gleaming coppers. Modern lorries still deliver to private customers, but a handful of ancient Citroën trucks and vans, of Delomel vintage, are still around and used for publicity. The workers in the brewery tend to gather in the small bar at the end of the working week, to sample the latest brew and pass on their comments to the head brewer, Norbert Kranz. Kranz started work as a sweeper-up in the brewery and has worked his way up. When there was a party to celebrate that 70th birthday, Francis Delomel, aged 95, was there, as was Roland Castelain, Yves, of course and his son Bertrand – four generations of brewers.

Each year, in late October or early November, the brewery is thrown open for the weekend to launch the annual Christmas beers. It is quite a party – not only is the whole of Bénifontaine there (all three hundred of them), but literally thousands turn up from all over the North of France.

Only one bit of nostalgia has been done away with – the miners' head has now faded away completely from the bottle labels and logos, so that the names of the beers stand out more clearly.

Brasserie La Choulette

16, rue des Ecoles
59111 Hordain
Tel: 03.27.35.72.44
Fax: 03.27.25.34.12

Hordain is between Valenciennes and Cambrai, south of the larger town of Bouchain. It is best approached from the N30, or the A1 Autoroute – Hordain is signposted from both roads. Turn left at the T junction in the village for the brewery, which is opposite the headquarters of the local brass band, the *Fanfare*. The brewery yard, through the gates, is sometimes cluttered, but there should be room. Head for the office, the *Acceuil*.

They still play *la crosse en plain* in a dozen or so villages around Maubeuge, to the east of Valenciennes. The game is recognisable as a primitive form of golf and involves belting a small oval wooden ball, *la choulette*, with a club, miles (or rather, kilometres) across open countryside. The game is described in long and loving detail by Emile Zola, in his magnificent novel, Germinal, which was based, in part, around research which the author had done in the mining community of Anzin, near Valenciennes. I once asked a group of players if they ever tried modern golf. "No", came the withering reply, "that is for bank managers and civil servants".

Alain Dhaussy named his brewery after the game and there are certain similarities of thought – he likes his history and traditions, just as the *la crosse* players do. The tasting room at the brewery has *la crosse* clubs and *choulettes* as decor – the room also has on display a splendid set of Dhaussy's traditional beers. The old print of the game on the bottle labels is, regrettably, being slowly faded away, because of the increasingly draconic French laws which forbid any association between alcohol and sport.

Monsieur Dhaussy's grandfather and great grandfather were brewers, not here in Hordain, but in nearby villages. He has an encyclopaedic knowledge of long-gone local breweries and beers – and even remembers being given weak beer with his school dinners. After a generation gap, he took up the mantle again, qualifying as a brewer in Douai, then buying what was the Bourgeois-Lecerf Brewery in 1977. The original brewery was built here in 1885. The Bourgeois-Lecerf Brewery had gone over to lager production in which proved to be a failed attempt to keep up with modern trends. Dhaussy gathered together equipment from other defunct breweries – his "new" coppers, which are superb, date from the 1920s and the whole place is a fascinating mix of ancient and modern.

He delved into the old Bourgeois-Lecerf recipe books and found an old Christmas beer which he liked the look of – the receipt was tweaked a little, then launched as *La Choulette Ambrée*, a strong amber beer (7.5% ABV) awash with caramel flavour, in 1981. Later, came *La Choulette Framboise*, which was the ambrée freshened up with natural raspberry extract, and *La Choulette Blonde*, sharp, clean, equally powerful and delicious. Alain Dhaussy is a keen student of national history and in 1986, introduced his *Bière des Sans Culottes*, as an expression of his approval of the French Revolution (The revolutionaries abolished the old sinecures and taxes which had allowed the rich to control brewing activities – the "sans culottes" were the people who wore smocks or trousers, as opposed to the "culottes", or silk breeches, of the aristos and courtiers). For the 200th anniversary of the Revolution in 1989, Citizen Dhaussy cranked up the beer to 8%ABV and called it *La Bière des Sans Culottes Brassin Robespierre*. "You should drink it in moderation", he says, "to make sure you escape the Terror". *L'Abbaye de Vaucelles*, another blonde at 7.5%, commemorates the foundation of that name, fragments of which survive 12 kilometres down the road south of Cambrai, at Les Rues des Vignes.

His latest creation (1996) is *La Tour d'Ostrevent*, a magnificent *bière de garde* which is wickedly smooth for a beer of its strength (8.3% ABV). Ostrevent was an ancient feudal territory, centred on Bouchain – the old central tower of the castle is preserved as a museum, with a collection of relics and mementoes from Merovingian times up until 1940, when a French army unit held out for several days against the German invaders.

In the cellar beneath the hospitality and tasting room, Monsieur Dhaussy has a small museum – a collection of old brewery equipment and memorabilia – which is well worth seeing. Even better if Monsieur Dhaussy can spare the time and explain some of the significance of the exhibits to you.

Brewery and museum visits, by prior arrangement, Monday to Friday. No charge. Take you chances if you turn up unannounced, although you can always buy beer, there may not be a spare body to show you round the place. Open Monday to Friday 0800-1200, 1400-1800. Saturday morning 0900-1200.

Although Hordain and Bouchain are largely red-brick reconstructions post-First World War devastation – and on the edge of the old mining belt – there is fascinating country around here. Alain Dhaussy is a leading light in the organisation which seeks to encourage tourism in the *Val de la Sensée*, a mysterious region of river, canal, meres and woodland. Arleux, famous for its wonderful peat-smoked garlic is not far away, as is Lecluse, a village where the poet Verlaine used to work and write. It is rumoured that behind the plaque which marks the cottage where he stayed, the workmen walled up a bottle of red wine. As far as they were concerned, Verlaine was remembered as the visiting village drunk. At Lewarde is the most visited museum in the North of France, the *Centre Historique Minier* (see separate entry under Lewarde). The new micro-brewery Cambier, at Aubigny-au-Bac, is even closer.

Brasserie De Clerck

42, rue Georges Clemenceau
80200 Peronne
Tel: 03.22.84.30.94
Fax: 03.22.84.26.76

Peronne is on the River Somme, some twenty five kilometres east of St-Quentin. The A1 Autoroute runs past the town to the west, the A26 to the east. The De Clerck Brewery has shop front, with beers and wines on display, on the main street of Peronne

41

– the Rue St-Sauveur – dive down the street at the side of the shop and you will find the brewery itself. The office is in a Portacabin in the brewery yard.

The big tourist attraction of Peronne is *L'Historial*, a superb and revelatory new museum which will tell you all you need to know about the First World War in general and the Battle of the Somme in particular. After your visit, I can assure you that you will be much shaken up and will need to get back in touch with present-day life. De Clerck's beers should do the trick.

The De Clerck family trace their brewing dynasty back to 1774, when Joannes De Clerck opened a brewhouse next door to his farm in the village of Hondeghem, near Hazebrouck, then in Flanders, now part of France. Several generations on, immediately after the First World War, the brewery passed to two brothers, Pierre and Gabriel De Clerck, who decided that the time had come for a change. In 1928, Pierre bought a brewery-maltery which had just been constructed in Peronne, while in 1932, Gabriel acquired a brewery nearer home, in Hazebrouck.

Pierre's decision to come to Peronne was a shrewd and brave one – the town had been on the front line for most of the war and had been all but obliterated. It was, according to one contemporary observer in 1918, "more of a geographical expression rather than a town". Serious thought was given to abandoning the place altogether and re-siting a new town on nearby Mount St-Quentin, but gradually life crept back.

Michel De Clerck, who retired very recently as *maitre-brasseur*, was born a couple of years before the move to Peronne and eventually took over from his father Pierre in 1975. Within a few years, there was a crisis, as both breweries came under pressure from the giant conglomerates who were threatening to overwhelm the smaller companies in Northern France. The Hazebrouck brewery, which had been modernised in the 1960s, was sold lock, stock and barrel in 1985 to an Australian entrepreneur, who shipped the machinery to Australia, where it is apparently still functioning. (It would be fascinating to know what sort of beer they are making).

In Peronne, Michel took the decision to hang on, to re-shape production and to go for the specialist beer market, which meant developing entirely new brands. The new beers were to be old-styled, culled from old family recipe books, brewed with tender loving care from the very best of regional materials, strong, flavoursome, individual. It was, he says, an interesting challenge for someone who had been steeped in the beer business from childhood – Monsieur De Clerck claims that he never tasted water until he was evacuated from Peronne during the Second World War, when he was fourteen.

Pot Flamand, a gentle caramelly amber beer at 7% ABV, made from dark Picard malts and French, Belgian and Czech hops, was the first in line. As the name suggests, the recipe came from Hazebrouck. Like all Monsieur De Clerck's beers, it is bottom fermented. There is an eight week period of secondary fermentation and maturation – *le temps de garde* – then follows filtration and bottling. Pot Flamand is also sold under the name of **La Belle Siska** – the latter name seems to be used more often these days.

In 1986, he came up with what proved to be a winner – **La Colvert**, a fine *bière blonde*, again at 7% ABV, made with pale malts and predominantly aromatic Saaz hops. I think what pushes up the sales in Picardy, besides its undoubted quality, is the name and the label. "Colvert" means mallard and the picture on the bottle, from a charming original painting by Monsieur De Clerck himself, depicts the aforementioned duck in flight, plus a fisherman at work from his punt. Fishing and shooting are twin obsessions of many folk along the river Somme and its adjacent *étangs*, or meres.

The trio is completed by **La Fanette**, which is a golden beer, at a comparatively modest 5.5% ABV. Monsieur De Clerck does not follow the recently rediscovered fashion of producing a *bière de mars* or a *bière de Noël* – he says simply that La Fanette is suitable for Spring and La Belle Siska is appropriate for Christmas, but they are both for sale, together with Colvert, to be enjoyed all the year round. All three beers are soft and gentle, with the emphasis much more on malt than hop. I think it is no coincidence that they are all feminine names. Madame Eliane De Clerck, Michel's wife has been extremely influential in the development of the brewery over the last few crucial years – she now runs the whole operation. Production at the brewery runs at 5000 hectolitres per year.

It is not possible to visit the brewery; it is a complex, dark, place, with low ceilings and the old copper brewing kettles projecting through two floors. Fine if you know your way around, but visitors could easily get lost. You can, however, buy the beers from the office. *Office opening hours are Monday - Friday, 0800-1200, 1330-1700.* If you happen to be staying at the Hostellerie des Ramparts, a Logis de France Hotel in Peronne where many British tourists spend a first or last night within striking distance of the ferry ports, you will find that De Clerck's beers are available.

Brasserie Duyck

113, rue Nationale
59144 Jenlain
Tel: 03.27.49.70.03
Fax: 03.27.49.74.81

The name of the village, and the beer, Jenlain, is better known, world-wide, than the name of the brewery. Jenlain is about 10 kilometres east of Valenciennes, on the D934, which used to be a *rue Nationale*, but has now been bypassed by the N49 between Valenciennes and Bavay. From the direction of Valenciennes, come off the N49 for Curgies, turn right for Jenlain. You will see the brewery, on the left, before you get to Jenlain village. There is a large car and lorry park right next door to the brewery. Head for the Acceuil, which is though the gates and immediately on the right.

Michael Jackson's World Guide to Beer (1977) has a wonderful photograph of two members of the Duyck family, dressed in no-nonsense boots and overalls, carrying a wooden beer barrel slung on a pole on their shoulders. They stand before their farmhouse, a solid brick-built building of 1840, which, Jackson wrote "overlooks the brewery". Times have changed for the Brasserie Duyck. The brewery has been modernised and expanded – the farmhouse is till there, but it would be fair to say that nowadays, the brewery overlooks the farmhouse. There are no wooden barrels, and I doubt very much if Raymond Duyck, the present owner, even owns a pair of boots and overalls. In the 1970s, production at the brewery was 15000 hectolitres. Now, according to the latest figures, it is 75000 – and 95% of that is the remarkable beer known as Jenlain.

The latest publicity brochures for Jenlain are extremely sleek and sophisticated, and talk of "quatre generations d'un secret bien gardé". The four generations cover Léon Duyck, who was a farmer-brewer in Zeggers-Cappel, in Flanders, his son Félix, who moved from Flanders to Jenlain to found a new brewery in 1922, his grandson Robert, who named the old *bière de garde* Jenlain in the 1960s and presided over the expansion of the brewery in the 1980s, and his great-grandson Raymond, who took over in 1990. Jenlain is hardly a "well-kept secret" these days – it is the best-known *bière de garde* in France, and sells all over the beer-drinking world.

Very recently, the brewery got together with the publishers of the prestigious Gault-Millau restaurant guide to produce *Le Guide des Ambassadeurs Jenlain* – a list of up-market bars and restaurants, all over France, which offer Jenlain. The pamphlet is included in the annual Gault-Millau guide and the participating establishments display a neat enamel plaque announcing the fact.

Jenlain (6.5% ABV), a rich *ambrée-going-on-rousse* colour, is made with a variety of malts from Flanders, Champagne and Burgundy, and four varieties of hop, from France, Belgium, Germany and Slovenia, is top-fermented, given forty days *garde*, filtered, but not pasteurised. It still appears most familiarly in the traditional champagne-type bottle, but is also available in 33 and 25cl crown-capped bottles, in 50cl tins, and on draught.

In 1994, the brewery introduced a new *bière blonde*, **Sebourg** (6% ABV), named after a village just to the north of Jenlain. Pale malt from Champagne, together with a small amount of Beauce wheat, and Alsace hops are used. The Sebourg connection would appear to be that the wheat used is ground at a water mill in Sebourg. (There were no less than three breweries in the village in the 1930s and it is claimed that the new Duyck recipe was a springtime *bière de garde* discovered in one of the old Sebourg brewery recipe books). Sebourg is available in bottle and on draught – the *Bière Fraîche*, only on sale on draught at the brewery's showcase Cafe Jenlain, in the centre of Lille, is Sebourg, unfiltered.

There are seasonal *bières de garde* – a *bière de Noël*, very close to Jenlain, but slightly stronger, at 6.8% ABV, and, since 1991, a *bière de Printemps*, at 5.4% ABV. Le DB is a lager, only on draught, named after General Leclerc's division "Le 2eDB", which liberated Jenlain in 1944. A new beer, La Fraîche de L'Aunelle, was introduced in 1998 (see Tasting Notes).

You can't tour the brewery, but you can buy the beers at the office – the procedure is to pay for what you want (usually by the case), then take the receipt into the brewery to collect. That way you can at least sniff the air and see part of the bottling plant. The office is open 0800 – 1200 and 1400 – 1700 Monday to Thursday – closes at 1600 on Fridays. Closed Saturday and Sunday.

Entre-Temps

1 place de la Gare
59306 Valenciennes
Tel: 03.27.46.86.30
Open every day 0630 – 2230

The station buffet is invariably a reliable place to eat in France – in Valenciennes, as from December 1997, it is also an interesting place to drink. The equipment was provided by BBG, a company who are based in Villeneuve d'Ascq, near Lille. Key members of the company used to work at the Pelforth brewery, until it was taken over by Heineken.

Their neat, small, Pico 150 brewery can produce 150 litres of top-fermented beer a day, six days a week, for 330 days a year. The beers are fermented for three days, then given a minimum of seven days *garde*. The same firm installed the same equipment at the Café-Restaurant de la Poste, in St-Pol-sur-Ternoise, and the Taverne de l'Ecu in Lille. (See separate entries).

The draught *Bière de la Maison* here is a top-fermented *bière blanche*, at 5.5% ABV, although that could change and you could find yourself drinking a *blonde*, an *ambrée*, or a *brune*, while waiting for a train. Try a baked potato and filling, and a beer, at 25F. The music here is a cut above the rest.

Les Brasseurs de Gayant

63 Faubourg de Paris
59502 Douai
Tel: 03.27.93.26.22
Fax: 03.27.93.26.20

From the centre of Douai, find the ring road and from the Place L'Hérillier (where the Boulevard Pasteur meets the Boulevard Paul Hayez), follow the signs for the N43 to Cambrai. Once over the railway bridge, look out for a small wooded patch on the left – there is a tiny sign for the brewery here. Turn sharp left at the sign, then right into the wastelands of the Faubourg de Paris. The brewery office is in the modern block on the left.

The Brasseurs de Gayant is a new name for the brewery formerly known as La Brasserie des Enfants de Gayant. I'm not sure what the change of title means, but the marketing men must have an explanation; the key word remains Gayant. The Gayant is the Giant of Douai (Gayant being the way they spelled géant back in the 16th century, when the carnival giant first made his appearance). The Gayant, not to mention his wife and children, is an important central figure in the town's history and pysche, and has a three day festival each year – Douai is familiarly known as the *cité de Gayant*, its citizens as *les enfants de Gayant*.

The origins of the brewery go back to 1919, when four local breweries, Hollande-Beauvois, Lallart-Maronnier, Delfolie and Caudrelier, joined forces to create La Grand Brasserie Co-opérative des Enfants de Gayant on the Faubourg de Paris site. Jean-Pierre d'Aubréby bought the brewery in 1955 and in the 1970s produced a non-alcoholic beer, La Celta Brune, which enjoyed huge success nationwide. The brewery was modernised in the 1980s largely from the proceeds of La Celta Brune.

Jean-Pierre's son, Patrick d'Aubréby, took charge in 1987, by which time a new tide – towards powerful *bières de specialité* – was flowing. Since the early 1990s, there has been a micro-brewery within the brewery, under the direction of Alain Dessy, a Belgian, whose task it is to produce a new beer every two years or so. There is now a considerable portfolio of interesting beers, to go with the likes of the Saaz Old Lager and the Celta. Total production at the brewery is now 200,000 hectolitres per year, which makes them the sixth largest French brewery.

La Bière du Desert is a strong (7% ABV) lager, first brewed to celebrate the Paris-Dakar car rally in 1986.

Next came *L'Abbaye de St-Landelin*, which appeared first as a *blonde*, but is now available as *ambrée* and *brune*. This is advertised as *l'unique bière de L'Abbaye française*. The original notion of the recipe came from a small, now defunct brewery, the Brasserie Rimaux, which used to produce a top-fermented beer called Réserve St-Landelin. (Michael Jackson mentions the Brasserie Rimaux in his World Guide to Beer, 1977). The brewer claimed an inspiration going back to the abbey brewery at Crespin, which had ceased to function before the French Revolution – the abbey had been founded by St Landelin's spring. I have heard stories of the Brasserie Rimeaux, whose brewing methods and measurements were fairly basic – a sackful of this, a handful of that; I am sure the Gayant version is a careful and highly scientific version of the old. *L'Abbaye de St-Landelin Triple Brune* (8% ABV) was added to the list in 1997.

La Bière du Démon, introduced in 1990, is aptly named, since it is 12% ABV and was claimed at the time of its appearance to be the strongest *blonde* in the world. That record would now appear to belong to the Brasserie Jeanne d'Arc's Belzebuth.

In 1994, came what has been to date the most successful of the new beers, *La Goudale* (7.5% ABV), a top-fermented pale *bière de garde*, which has an even more torturous historical lineage than St-Landelin. The 14th century recipe, it is claimed, came from *les vieux grimoires* of the library in Douai – since "grimoires" translates as "magician's book of spells", or "unreadable scribble", I think we can safely assume that Alain Dessy improvised on a theme. "Goudale" would appear to be the French for "Good Ale" – a goud tale. And it *is* an excellent beer. They sold two million bottles of it in 2 years.

The latest beer is *Amadeus*, a top-fermented *bière blanche sur lie*, at 4.5% ABV. This is brewed *dans le pur respect de la méthode des moines de l'abbaye de Crespin* – a bit more homage to those monks at St-Landelin's spring at Crespin.

Brasserie Heineken

Rue du Houblon
ZI de la Pilaterie
59370 Mons-en-Baroeul
Tel: 03.20.33.67.00
Fax: 03.20.33.68.70

You have to be pretty determined to find the Heineken brewery, since it involves negotiating the Lille high-speed or ring-roads, usually white-knuckle rides. From Lille centre, follow the *Voie Rapide* towards Roubaix, coming off at the sign for the ZI de la Pilaterie. From the A22, leave at the *Echange de Croix-Mons-en-Baroeul*, again following the ZI sign. The Rue de la Couture joins two roundabouts, one at either end of the Zone Industrielle. The Rue de Houblon crosses the Rue de la Couture – take the southern end for the brewery. The scenery is exactly what you might expect in a modern industrial estate.

Heineken do organise tours of the brewery (in French, English or German), from Monday to Friday each week, but you have to book in advance, either as a group, or as an individual, by agreeing to join a group. If you don't have an appointment, you won't even get in the car park. Ring Monsieur Hervé Cousin's office, sort yourself out and they will even provide you with a map beforehand.

Everything here is on a gigantic scale – a vast site, fermenting vessels they call Apollo's because they are the size of American space-rockets, a bottling plant which churns out 70000 bottles an hour, a total annual production of three million hectolitres. The tour, smartly led by girls in air-hostess uniforms, is extremely efficient and takes two and a half hours, up and down stairs, along walkways high above the action, punctuated by videos which explain what is going on.

What is not explained is Heineken's swift and devastating progress from an exporter (via French distribution companies), to a massive player within the French brewing industry. They bought out the Alsacienne de Brasserie group (Albra), in 1976. Albra was itself a 1969 merger between the Brasserie d'Espérance (Schlitigheim), Perle (also Schlitigheim). Colmar (Colmar), Haag (Ingwiller) and Mutzig (Mutzig). Heineken used Albra as a distributing arm at first, but in 1980, took the decision to start brewing in France, at Schlitigheim.

In 1984, there was a merger between Heineken and the Union des Brasseries (another French conglomerate which included companies in Chalons-sur-Marne, Marseille, Lyon, Alsace and the French colonial company, Brasseries et Glacières de l'Indochine). This latter had, since 1980, a controlling interest in Pelforth, in Lille. In 1992, Heineken emerged as sole owners and controllers, having already expanded and modernised the Lille plant.

Heineken means more Heineken for a grateful world, of course, but along the way they have also preserved some of the more successful brands of their victims. The present portfolio includes 22 labels, several of them from the original Pelforth company. Time for more back-tracking.

The Brasserie du Pélican traced its roots back to the 1860s, and to Loos, just outside Lille – Pasteur was a famous consultant to the brewery. Real power came after the First World War, after a three-way merger. The name Pélican was taken from a popular fox-trot of the day and was also given to a new beer, a Pils-type lager, first produced in 1921.

In 1937, the brewery introduced Pelforth Brune, a strong brown ale, deliberately based on the English pattern – the name was a contraction of Pélican-forte, strong Pélican. In the 1960s, Pélican/Pelforth co-sponsored a team in the *Tour de France* – they won, in 1968. Hence came the slogan "Donnez une brune aux hommes qui ont soif" – "Pelforth brown helps you win the Tour de France". Production soared, and the brewery was renamed Pelforth in 1972.

The company had another unusual beer on the menu – George Killian's, an originally top-fermented "red" *bière Irlandaise*. Life is too short for an exhaustive study of the genealogy of George Killian's. Briefly, it began life as an Irish beer brewed by George Killian Lett, of Enniscorthy, County Wexford; he stopped brewing in the mid 1950s, but kept the license to the name, which was leased out to Pelforth in France and Coors in the USA. Pelforth launched it in a big way in France in 1972 (the Coors version would appear to be completely different), and is now accepted as a "traditional" beer of the North of France. George Killian's is now bottom-fermented. Pelforth Blonde was launched only in 1991 – "a little sister for the brown" – as the promotion put it. The "traditional" *bière de Noël de Pelforth* dates from 1986, the *bière de mars Pelforth* from 1996. A wonderful thing, tradition.

So, to cut a long story sideways, the northern French beers which Heineken still produce at Mons-en-Baroeul are *Pélican* (a lager at 4.8% ABV, in the traditional litre bottle, with swing-top porcelain stopper), *Pelforth Brune and Blonde* bottled and on draught, the Pelforth spring and Christmas beers, and *George Killian's*. (Although word is that George Killian's is now brewed at the Heineken plant in Marseille). There is also ***Porter 39, "La Brune du Nord"***, an English-style porter originally brewed in Maubeuge in 1929, swept up by the Union de Brasseries group, then by Heineken.

There are a couple of moments on the inter-planetary-space-station Heineken tour when history butts in. The old central Pélican/Pelforth brewing hall, overlooked by an image of St Arnould, is the setting for a bizarre *son-et-lumière* show which appears to be a dialogue between the saint and the yeast-fairy about the magic of fermentation. (I couldn't help laughing out loud at this, which caused some consternation with my guide. She said *all* of her British customers laughed at this point and she couldn't understand why. I had to try and explain that the cut-glass Home-counties accents of the actors made it sound like Listen with Mother – but then my French floundered at the attempt to explain Listen with Mother.) The hall though, with its cathedral like proportions, gleaming coppers and spotless tiled walls, *is* impressive. They offer free drinks at the end of the tour – most people take Heineken, but I asked for and got the Pelforth Brune – and that's still an impressive drink.

The Heineken juggernaut is still rolling through the north. In 1996, they took control of the St-Omer Brewery (not to mention Fischer, in Alsace). There is a separate entry in this book for the Brasserie St-Omer – Heineken have promised to keep their beer repertoire in situ and on stream for three years.

Brasserie Jeanne D'Arc

38 rue Anatole France
59790 Ronchin
Tel: 03.20.16.92.92.
Fax: 03.20.88.26.01

Ronchin is on the south-eastern outskirts of Lille. Leave the A1 at exit 20 for Ronchin, follow the signs for Lille. After you have passed the city boundary, look out for a railway bridge which crosses the road – after you have gone under the bridge, turn right into the narrow road which becomes the Rue Anatole France. The brewery is on the left, some way down this road and hiding behind large wrought-iron gates. The car park might be a squeeze, but there is usually a place or two.

At the very end of the nineteenth century, Ronchin was a small agricultural town of 3500 people – and five breweries. Monsieur Henri Vandamme owned one of them, but in 1898, he secured financial backing to move to a new site, to found an "industrial" brewery. Vandamme was clearly very shrewd, for he had sensed that the old-style farm breweries were of out of date and in Ronchin he was perfectly placed to exploit the thirst of Lille, while remaining close to his sources of barley in the surrounding countryside. (It is hard to imagine countryside nowadays in Ronchin – most of the place has been completely swallowed up by the urban tide).

At every stage, Vandamme's successors seemed to make just the right moves at just the right time.

Desire Desruelle, first a partner, then a successor, sent out salesmen to hunt up new trade in 1906 – very early days in the marketing game. Desruelle owned agricultural land in Lomme, another town on the outskirts of Lille. As he sold the land off for residential building, he always kept the corner sites to himself, to build estaminets, which would be supplied by the brewery. He started selling beer in bottles in 1912 – long before most of his rivals had even considered the idea.

The brewery was ransacked by the Germans during the First World War, but Desruelle had it up and running again by 1919. Around about 1927, the brewery became known as the Brasserie Jeanne D'Arc – they had been using pictures of St-Joan on their bottles for several years. Desruelle died in 1938 and control finally passed to his son-in-law, Charles Leclercq, whose ancestors had been brewers since the seventeenth century. Leclercq, and his technical director, Pierre Decarne, were almost certainly responsible for the introduction and marketing of one of the brewery's famous beers, Scotch Triumph, a strong, bottom-fermented brown beer, which won prizes at exhibitions and competitions all over

Europe in the 1930s and is still part of the company's repertoire.

Leclercq saw the business through the difficult days of the Second World War, when they were reduced to making a feeble beer with sugarbeet. In 1945, a time when many brewers gave up, he actually bought more land to extend the brewery. In the 1960s he diversified into sodas and lemonades.

In the 1990s, his sons, Dominique and Bruno oversaw a doubling of the brewery's production of *bières spécialites*, while making an important penetration of British supermarkets with a cheap lager, Pilsor, while still retaining an unusual number of private clients. A very clever dynasty, the Vandammes, Desruelles and Leclercqs. The Brasserie Jeanne D'Arc is the tenth largest in France, and produces 100,000 hectolitres a year.

The cast of the most interesting beers, in order of appearance, begins with *Scotch Triumph*, in 1936, and continues with *Orpal*, a pale lager at 5.2% ABV, introduced in 1949. (Very recently, the brewery has been using the name Orpal to market all their beers, although they retain the Jeanne D'Arc name in lower case).

In 1984 came *Gold Triumph*, another bottom-fermented *blonde*, slightly stronger than Orpal. The 1990s saw the birth of the *Ambre de Flandres* (6.4% ABV), a bottom-fermented *bière de garde*, and *Grain D'Orge*, a top-fermented *bière de garde* of 8% ABV, in the traditional 75cl corked bottle. They are extremely proud of the fact that Grain D'Orge won the Gold Medal in the *bière de garde* category at the World Beer Cup International, in Colorado, USA, in 1996.

The latest recruit, apparently encouraged by the Italian market, is *Belzebuth*, a ferocious (and record-breaking) top-fermented *blonde*, at an incredible 15% ABV. Belzebuth, or Beelzebub, was, you may remember, the price of the devils and second in rank to Satan himself. The beer is sold in 25cl bottles and should be taken in small doses.

There are seasonal beers, a *bière de mars* and a *bière de Noël*, both introduced, says the brewery, in the 1970s.

Le Moulin à Bière

Cité de l'Europe
62231 Coquelles
Tel: 03.21.85.30.02
Fax: 03.21.36.02.63

The Cité de l'Europe, near Coquelles, just south of Calais, is a very strange place indeed. A maze of new, narrow black-top roads and rusticated roundabouts, overlooked by lamp standards which resemble wilting black daffodils, surround a corrugated aluminium aircraft hangar which houses multiplex cinemas and a colossal shopping mall, with parking for 3500 vehicles. (Paul Andrew, a British architect, is responsible for this moonscape).

If you are using the Shuttle, this is where you arrive and depart. If you approach from inland France, leave the A16 at exit 12 or 14, ignore the derelict but prominent windmill (moulin) on the outskirts of the village, ignore the village of Coquelles, and follow the bewildering signs for the Cité and the Centre Commercial. The Moulin à Bière is in the basement of the shopping mall.

There are a dozen major stores and 150 boutiques in the building, spread over two floors. (See Gazeteer for further details). Even experienced shopoholics begin to wilt after a time – they then head for the restaurants and fast food outlets. Down in the basement, there is a fake village square, with real fountain burbling over plastic rocks, surrounded by bars. To the left of this bizarre operatic set is an Irish bar (Flanagans), to the right there is a British pub (The John Bull), in the centre is the Moulin à Bière, one of the new generation of French brew-pub/restaurants, opened by Monsieur Bernard Happiete in 1995.

Just so that you know where you are, there is a finger-post in the large and often busy bar which points to the *salle de brassage* (the brew-house), the *salle de fermentation* and the *salle de garde*, not to mention *Le Tunnel* (100 metres). It is all bright, clean, fast and modern, so it is odd to see murals of French everyday beer and brewing life c1800, decorating the walls.

Try the *Palette Dégustation*, a tray of three or four small glasses called *galopins*, each with a sample of the brewery's output. All the beers are top-fermented, made with three or four varieties of hop, unfiltered and unpasteurised and surprisingly good. There is a *blonde* (5.5% ABV), a *blanche* (4.5% ABV), an *ambrée* (6% ABV) and a *brune* (6.4% ABV), with seasonal beers at the appropriate times of the year. Having alighted upon a favourite, you may graduate to *la pinte* (which turns out to be 25cl), *le middle* (33cl), *la chope* (50cl), *le géant* (1.1 litres), and *le big mill* (1.8 litres).

There are takeaway versions of all the draught beers, in 75cl bottles or 5 litre canisters, all ridiculously over-priced. The bottles do not travel well and the beers within go off alarmingly quickly.

Beer cocktails are on offer – *L'Eméraude* (Curacao, Tequila, Beer), *Le Dynamite* (Whisky and beer) and *Le Détonnant* (bière flambée, secret de la maison) – they would surely only tempt those driven suicidal by shopping abuse. The house beers are the only beers – there is no list of bottled beer.

Food is actually quite good and compares more than favourably with the offerings of the other restaurants in the Cité. The staple diet would appear to be *flammekeuches*, which are pizza-based creations with a variety of different toppings, and *choucroutes* – both of which are guaranteed to increase thirst and therefore beer consumption. You can combine both with the very reasonable *Formule Moulin* (89F), which gives you a *flammekeuche*, a *choucroute* and a 25cl slug of one of the house beers.

All in all, an interesting experience. The only temptations next door in the John Bull, a splendid reproduction Edwardian pub (Tetleys and Ind Coup keg beers on draught), are the dart board and immaculate bar billiards table.

The Moulin à bière is open every day from 1000 – 2400.

Café Restaurant de la Poste

16 place General Leclerc
62130 St-Pol-sur-Ternoise
Tel: 03.21.03.35.87

Open every day, from 0900. Closing times vary, but usually about 2100. Restaurant open every lunchtime and evening.

A new micro, opened in November 1997, with equipment from BBG. The draught beer here at St-Pol is called *La Polopolitaine* (the name given to the inhabitants of the town), and is at the moment a *bière blanche* at 5.5% ABV. The whole enterprise – café, restaurant and brewery – is run by Bruno and Marie-France Guilbert. There are now two new micro breweries in St-Pol – this one and St-Poloise.

De la Poste is, surprise, surprise, near the Post Office. Don't be put off by the Heineken signs – *everyone* is drinking the new fresh-brewed bière blanche.

Brasserie de St-Omer

9 rue Edouard-Devaux
62500 St-Omer
Tel: 03.21.98.76.00
Fax: 03.21.88.57.50

The Brasserie de St-Omer is best approached on foot, via the Rue de Dunkerque, which runs downhill from the main square of St-Omer, the Place du Maréchal Foch. If it isn't market day (Saturday morning), you should be able to park in the central square, outside the Hôtel de Ville. Parking around the brewery itself is possible but tricky.

Heineken took a controlling interest in the Brasserie de St-Omer in 1996. In one sense, there was an improvement, since Heineken instigated an improved and highly organised tourist policy for the brewery – *ring Monsieur Mercier, 03.21.38.68.68 for details and an appointment.* On the other hand, one wonders what will happen next. Heineken have promised to "preserve the identity" of the Brasserie de St-Omer for three years.

The problem is trying to sort out what exactly the identity of the St-Omer brewery was in the first place. Its history is complicated enough, and a textbook exercise in the recent frenetic contractions of the French brewing industry. Prior to 1985, this was the Brasserie Artésienne, which had originally been founded in St-Omer in 1866. They were bought out and renamed the Brasserie de St-Omer by the group Saint-Arnould (GSA), who were essentially wine merchants and bottling contractors. GSA later took over the Brasserie Facon at Pont-de-Briques, near Boulogne, the Brasserie Semeuse at Hellemmes in Lille, and the Brasseries des Coopérateurs in Solesmes, Sin-le-Noble and Denain.

In the end, the St-Omer site was modernised and expanded, everywhere else was closed, although some of the beers retained. Production at St-Omer soared from 60000 hectolitres in 1986 to 1,400,000 hectolitres in 1996. Heineken bought a majority interest in GSA – and here we are.

The tour of the brewery is interesting enough although, apart from a line of comparatively venerable copper mash tuns overlooking the street, everything else is space-age, computer controlled, all but incomprehensible and utterly without character. The modern bottling line, over the road from the main brewery, is a big tourist draw – if you have never seen (or been deafened by) a bottling line before, then you may well find it fascinating.

There is still a long line of beers, all of them bottom-fermented, Pils-type or *bières de luxe*, including Bière Saint-Omer (5% ABV), Facon de Luxe (5.2% ABV), La Semeuse (5% ABV), Nordik Extra Lager (5.9% ABV). There is an impressive tasting room, divided up into individual booths, in the bottling-plant side of the brewery. They tell me the tasters can actually tell the difference between these brands – they are obviously highly skilled men and women.

Slightly more interesting are *L'épi de Facon* (5.5% ABV) which is a bottom-fermented *blonde* with added wheat, and *La Réserve du Brasseur*, which is a bottom-fermented *bière de garde*, an *ambrée* at 6.4% ABV, only available on draught.

Brasserie St Poloise

2, rue de la Calandre
62130 Saint-Pol-sur-Ternoise
Tel and Fax: 03.21.41.91.00

St-Pol-sur-Ternoise nowadays is bypassed by the N39 Le Touquet-Arras road, but heavy traffic still groans through the place heading north to Lens or Lille and south to Amiens. The Brasserie St Poloise is hidden in a back street, away from the town centre. The easiest approach is from the D343, which goes towards Wavrons-sur-Ternoise from St Pol. Turn right into the Rue de la Calandre. There are small parking areas in front of the brewery and on the other side of the road.

The Brasserie St Poloise is a brasserie in both senses of the word – a brewery and a restaurant. It has been a long time coming, but worth the wait. Yves Castelain entered into negotiations with the local authorities in St Pol a couple of years ago, encouraged by the mayor, Philippe Vasseur, who was also a *deputé* and the then Minister of Agriculture, no less. (He was a casualty in President Chirac's disastrous snap election in 1997). The first beer, St-Poloise, appeared before the brewery did, brewed at Bénifontaine, but offered at a *fête des terres* in St Pol in 1996.

The brewery opened, with great ceremony, in June 1997. There were bands, street processions, a parade of vintage cars – and the Ghilde des Eswards Cervoisiers arrived in full costume and with banner flying, on a horse-drawn brewer's dray. Monsieur Vasseur cut the ribbon – a hop-bine – with a pair of secateurs. Visitors were offered a free badged glass and a tasting of the beer – three thousand of them took advantage of the offer. St Pol had seen nothing like it for years. You can still buy a beautifully made enamel plaque, or a T-shirt, to commemorate the occasion.

The transformation of the building – the old town abattoir – is impressive. You pass the shiny new brewery itself, a miniature symphony of copper and stainless steel, on the way to the bar; beyond that there are two fine rooms, one for what one might call regional fast-food, the other a place for more serious eating. (Menus between 79 and 129FF, available 1200-1430 and evenings. The whole place is closed on Mondays). Bertrand Castelain, Yves' son is in charge.

There are three beers, now all brewed at St Pol. *St Poloise Blonde* (6.4% ABV), on draught at the brewery, but mostly sold in 75cl bottles, is made from pale malts, with Northern Brewer hops from France, Saaz from Alsace. As with most Castelain beers, ale yeast is used at low temperatures, there is a period of *garde*, then a rough filtration. *The St Poloise Grand Cru* is slightly stronger, at 7% ABV. There is to be a St Pol Ambrée as well.

The label on the Blonde features a ravishing long-haired blonde, hefting a delicate fluted glass of beer, and announces "Houblon des Flandres". The Grand Cru is a more serious affair, with coat of arms and medallions. There is some amiable nonsense on the reverse side of the latter about a beer which "would not have disgraced the table of Louis de Luxembourg, Compte de St Pol in 1465, and was given to travellers by the local nunnery (Les Soeurs Noires) – and refreshed workers in the fields". I'm fairly relaxed about the Compte de St Pol and his ability to afford expensive beers, but the travellers and workers would have been pole-axed in fairly short order by a beer of this strength. Both are announced as beers *des Hautes de France*. Only a year or so ago, the people of the Nord-Pas de Calais rejected a notion to rename their territory "Hautes de France".

Let's not quibble with the eccentricities of advertising companies. The two beers, developed in 1996/7, are both magnificent and do not need instantly attached history and tradition to help them on their way.

Two new beers were introduced in 1998. *La Blanche de 7 Vallées* and *L'Ambrée des 7 Vallées* (see Tasting Notes).

There are tours of the brewery, by appoinment, and at a charge of 20F. (It's only 15F if you are part of a group of 15 or more). The tour includes a tasting and a souvenir.

The Abbaye de Belval, at Troisvaux, some five kilometres north of St-Pol, by the D87, is a restful and contemplative spot. There is a shop here which sells monastic produce – and one of the products is the splendid Belval cheese. This is a washed cheese – that is to say, the cheese rind is regularly washed during the process of ageing and refinement. The Sisters here now use St-Pol beer in that process.

Abbaye Notre-Dame de Belval
62130 Troisvaux
Tel: 03.21.04.10.10

Brasserie St Sylvestre

1, rue de la Chapelle
59114 Saint-Sylvestre-Cappel
Tel: 03.28.40.15.49
Fax: 03.28.40.13.44

Rue de la Chapelle, Saint-Sylvestre-Cappel – we are in France and Flanders. Saint-Sylvestre-Cappel is on the D916 from Dunkirk to Hazebrouck, 5 or 6 kilometres south-east of Cassel. The brewery is down the lane directly opposite the church. Parking is in front of the brewery office, or on the other side of the lane.

We are in the third generation of the Ricour family at St-Sylvestre. Remy Ricour inherited the brewery from his uncle in 1920 and handed over to his son, Pierre, in 1954. Pierre retired in 1985, having already seen through the launch of the pioneering and influential *bière de mars* (now known as *Bière Nouvelle*), which was to help preserve the brewery.

His sons, Serge and Christophe, introduced a new beer, *3 Monts*, in the same year. The Monts de Flandres are molehills of mountains, most of them less than 500 feet high, surging up unexpectedly in a soft and ravishing green countryside sprawled across the French-Belgian border. I am not certain exactly how many monts there are – there is certainly a cross-border cycle race every year, taking in nine of them. From the brewery, you can see three of them – the Mont des Cats, the Mont des Recollets and Mont Cassel – hence the name.

THE BREWERIES

3 Monts became, and remains, one of the very finest beers to come out of the recent revival of *bières de spécialité* in Northern France. It is a golden, top-fermented *bière de garde*, made with Brewers Gold and Hallertau hops (as are all the brewery's special beers) and two special (and secret) yeasts. Strength is 8.5% ABV and it is filtered, but not pasteurised. The label states proudly that it is a *Bière de Flandres*; Serge Ricour buys half of the total crop of hops grown in French Flanders each year. Each bottle also carries the *Excellences Pas-de-Calais* seal of approval. The reputation of 3 Monts has been spread almost entirely by word of mouth – not just in France.

One curiosity – the cork in the 75cl bottle has a deep v-shaped notch cut in the top of it and is held in place by a spring clip. Serge Ricour decided his "traditional" bottles had to look different and that was the difference. The clip can fly off in all sorts of directions when it is released and it can sometimes be difficult to twist off the corks from these champagne-style bottles, because you can't get a proper grip on them. You might need a corkscrew. It does sometimes make for a memorable experience.

The latest addition to the repertoire has been a long time coming – *Gavroche* was intended to arrive in 1989, to celebrate the bicentennial of the beginning of the French Revolution, but Serge Ricour is a tenacious and painstaking craftsman. He was not happy with the product in 1989 and was not going to be rushed – Gavroche was unveiled in 1997. It is a top-fermented *bière sur lie, rousse*, strong (8.5% ABV) and absolutely delicious. Presentation is in 33cl crown-capped bottles, each carrying a picture of the young boy Gavroche, a character in Victor Hugo's novel, Les Misérables.

At Christmas time, there is a rush for the St-Sylvestre *bière de Noël*, an *ambrée* made from pale, caramel and Munich malts, otherwise the same ingredients and processes as for 3 Monts. The brewery still makes a small quantity of bottom-fermented table beers, including Hoppeland bier Light (2% ABV), Hoppeland Bier (3.6%) and Luxe de Moulin (5%), but 70% of the entire production of 28000 hectolitres is given over to 3 Monts.

It is not possible in the normal course of events, to tour the brewery, which is a pity, because the material is a fascinating mix of pan-European technology from France, Germany and Great Britain. You will have to content yourself with the wonderful aromas which curl around the village on brewing days, and a visit to the office to buy beers, plus badged glasses.

Both the brewery and the office are closed on Saturday afternoons, and all day on Sunday and Monday. Best to avoid lunchtimes, too.

Taverne de L'Écu

9 rue Esquermoise
59800 Lille
Tel: 03.20.57.55.66
Fax: 03.20.57.95.55

The Rue Esquermoise runs north-west out of Lille's Grand'Place, the Place General de Gaulle. The numbering along the Rue Esquermoise is haywire – the Taverne de L'Écu, at number 9, is on the left, only a couple of minutes from the Grand'Place. Enter via a long corridor, then up the steps.

The Taverne de L'Écu has a long and colourful history as an entertainment venue. Records show that in 1850, it was a respectable *café-concert* – a bar with musical entertainment. A few years later, police dossiers indicate that it was not quite so respectable and was known for its collection of interesting ladies. In 1865 it was called L'Eldorado – again a *café-concert*, this time with facilities for displays of magic and physical fitness. By the end of the century, in alliance with a place across the road, it was a German-style beer garden and restaurant. In the 1960s it was an art-house cinema, which gradually descended into a blue-movie house. Rescued from oblivion in 1994, it emerged again as a bar-brasserie – the micro-brewery was added in 1997.

The Taverne is huge; first a large bar with a dazzling array of pan-European beertaps (Heineken, Pelforth Brune, Weickse Witte and Kwak, among others). Beyond the bar there is the barn-sized brasserie, above that another balconied eating space. Intimate it is not. There are times during the day when the staff seem to outnumber the customers. The new shiny copper and stainless steel brewery, installed by BBG, seems comparatively small in this vast space and can be contemplated from the bar.

The *bière maison*, in late 1997, was a refreshing top-fermented draught *bière blanche*, reasonably priced by central Lille standards and available in glasses ranging from 25cl to one litre pitchers. An *ambrée, blonde* and *brune* are promised. The extensive bottled beer list includes offerings from Germany, lots from Belgium and half a dozen good beers from Northern France. Thereafter, the beer menu declines into single sad international and fashionable examples such as Corona (Mexico), Budweiser (États Unis), Guiness (sic, Irlande) and Pilsner Urquell (Tcheque). The sole "English" beer is Martin's, which is Belgian.

Fast foods include *écuflettes*, which look pretty much like the *flammekueches* you get at the Moulin à Bière or Les 3 Brasseurs, *tavernettes*, which substitute a potato-cake base for the bread flour of the *écuflette*. There are *crêpes* (pancakes), *gaufres* (buckwheat pancakes) and a vast array of ice creams. *La Carte Brasserie* offers a choice of more substantial meals, including regional dishes like *Carbonade Flamande*, *Coq à la bière* and *Lapin à L'Artésienne*, which is rabbit cooked in beer.

La Taverne de L'Écu is open every day of the week, from 1100 – 2400 on Sunday, Monday and Tuesday, and from 1100 – 0200 Wednesday to Saturday inclusive.

Brasserie Terken

3 quai d'Anvers
59057 Roubaix
Tel: 03.20.26.92.26
Fax: 03.20.36.76.05

The *quai d'Anvers* was the Antwerp wharf, or quay, on the Roubaix canal, which separates Roubaix and

Tourcoing. Leave the A22 at exit 11, following the dual carriageway expressway sign-posted Roubaix/Wattrelos. The canal appears on the left, and eventually, you will see the brewery on the other side of the water. The huge white-on-blue panel "Terken" on top of the building looks at first sight like a motorway sign. Cross the canal by the bridge after the brewery and backtrack along the broad but decrepit and pot-holed towpath.

The Roubaix canal is in water, but effectively closed to traffic. With derelict locks and weed infested banks, it is a sad sight. Until comparatively recently, it was an important link in the French Inland Waterway system between Lille and Belgium, via the River Escaut, or Scheldt, and it made economic sense to have a canalside brewery. The Brasserie Co-opérative de Jean Guislain was established here at the beginning of the century.

After the First World War, the brewery merged with several others in the area and when it opened in 1920 after reconstruction and expansion, it was splendidly named the Grande Brasserie Moderne – GBM for short, GBM was a giant among the breweries of its time and production soared to 300,000 hectolitres a year in the 1930s. After World War Two, recovery was rapid and by the 1960s, production had doubled. The beers were delivered, mostly to private customers by a fleet of 50 lorries and 25 horse-drawn carts.

The brewery is now known as the Brasserie Terken. Sensible to change the name, for although it is an impressive collection of venerable buildings, it could not be described as especially "moderne". With production now running at 500,000 hectolitres per year, it is however, still the largest home-grown, home-owned brewery in Northern France (and the fourth largest in the country). Incredibly, a large proportion of production is still delivered to private customers, either from the brewery itself, or via its distribution centres in other areas. Those customers have also had the pleasure of a Christmas beer, actually anglicised as Christmas Ambrée, since 1948.

The range of bottled beers is enormous, but not especially interesting – they have had some success in exporting not-very-special lagers to British supermarkets. (Asda Bière de Luxe, Brueg, Upstall and Noordheim). The best known beers in France are Terken Blonde (5.2% ABV) and Terken Brune (6.7% ABV), which are available on draught and in small bottles.

Their connoisseurs' beer is **Septante-Cinq**, a bottom-fermented *bière de garde* of enthralling complexity, made with pale, caramel and torrified malts and Flemish Brewers' Gold, Northern Brewer, Strisselspalt, Hallertau and Tettnang hops. It comes out at 7.5% ABV and is magnificently presented in a corked and wired 75cl bottle. Septante-cinq is the Belgian-French simplified version of soixante-quinze (75) and I assume it refers to the bottle size.

The *bière de printemps*, introduced in 1995, is a *blonde au froment* 6.2% ABV), a pale beer with some wheat added. In 1997, the Brasserie Terken produced La Stout Terken, a dark, almost black "stoot" of 5.2% ABV, available at the moment only on draught in selected bars and cafés.

There are tours of the brewery, but they are sporadic and for organised groups, usually locals, customers or professionals. This is a shame, because it is a fascinating place with an extraordinary mix of architectural styles. It has to be said that the brewery is not very good at publicity, or at answering letters.

Brasserie Theillier

11 rue de la Chaussée
59570 Bavay
Tel and Fax: 03.27.63.10.18

Bavay is bypassed by the N49, between Valenciennes and Maubeuge. The town also has its own miniature ring road – follow this (to the right if coming from Valenciennes) until you find the D932 signposted right for Le Cateau. (There is a tiny brown sign here, which announces Brasserie Theillier). The brewery is 150 metres down this road, on the left. It is unmarked and quite difficult to spot, even when you are on top of the place – you might just glimpse the brewery yard through the gates. If the yard is not cluttered with crates and vehicles, there might be room to park.

The brewery is a small family-run affair and is open Monday to Friday, and Saturday mornings "unless there is a fête". Having said that, it is politic not to disturb family lunch on any day of the week. Brewing day is Friday.

The Theillier's have been brewing here since the 1850s – Michel, who took over from his father Armand in 1996, is the seventh generation of the family to work at Bavay. They trace their ancestry way back even further, to the Sires of Louvignies, the aristocrats who inhabited the now-vanished chateau down the road; the Theillier's rescued the worn stone-carved family arms and placed it above the entrance to the brew-house, and they use the same insignia on their bottle labels.

When I first found the place, several years ago, Armand and his wife, Janine, were in sole charge – and they had extraordinary tales to tell. The coppers are of 1918 vintage, installed with *dommages de guerre* – the Germans had taken away the originals. (There are family stories of German depredations during the Franco-Prussian War in 1870). Armand learned the trade the hard way from his grandfather during the Second World War, while his father was a prisoner of war. He subsequently brewed here for fifty years. They survived takeovers, he said, because they were "always one step behind with modernisation". Armand and Janine still live in the house right next door to the brewery.

The brewery today is an amazing place – old coppers, once coal-fired, now gas, conical fermentation tanks, stainless steel maturation vessels, computer-controlled processes, all crammed in a strange, dark, cramped ancient building.

Monsieur Theillier took me to the bottom of the garden, to point out one of the secrets of the success of the brewery – some way away, across fields, was their water source, a spring, flowing since Roman times. They also brewed, he said "à l'Anglais" – by decoction. Their old markets –

schools, factories, hospitals, private customers – began to dwindle in the late 1970s. Their salvation was a beer called **La Bavaisienne**, which emerged in its present form in the early 1980s. It had been part of the repertoire before the Second World War, as a *bière de mars*, at a comparatively light 4% ABV – it was increased in strength to 7% ABV.

The ingredients of La Bavaisienne are simple – pale malt from winter barley, and Brewers' Gold hops from Alsace. The beer, which is magnificent, rich, malty, sweet on the palate, bitter in the finish, suggests extraordinary complexities. It may be the water, the yeast, a long boil with pale malt, a long period of primary fermentation, a couple of months of *garde* – they are all Armand Theillier's secrets, now handed on to Michel.

There are other beers – *a bière Bock* (3.3% ABV), a *bière de Luxe* (4.6% ABV), which is a bottom-fermented Pils-lager (still, unaccountably the brewery's best-seller) and, for the first time in 1996, a *bière de Noël* (7% ABV).

For reasons which I have never been able to fathom, the beers are not available in any of the local cafes – best to buy at the brewery and take them home for mature reflection.

The 75cl crown-capped bottles of Bavaisienne are roughly filtered and have some lees left in the bottle – this is a much tastier version of the beer. The small 25cl bottles are clearer, cleaner – and not nearly so interesting.

Brasserie Thiriez

22, rue de Wormhout
59470 Esquelbecq
Tel and Fax: 03.28.62.88.44

The A25 Autoroute, from Dunkirk to Lille, is still toll-free and therefore sometimes busy. Signs tell you that *Vous êtes en Flandres* and display an encouraging symbol of a hop cone. Come off for Wormhout, some twenty five kilometres from the sea, and Esquelbecq is only minutes away. Approaching Esquelbecq from Wormhout, the Brasserie Thiriez is on the left, at the beginning of a sharp right-hand bend into the village. It looks like a farm rather than a brewery, but there is a sign. Turn left into the lane on the near side of the brewery, then look for the entrance right into the brewery/farm yard.

The guide books list the massive pink-brick and honeystone sixteenth century *église-halle*, or *hallekerke* (In Flanders, everything is described in French and Flemish) and the seventeenth century chateau. St Folquin's church was almost lost twenty or so years ago, when there was a fire which left only the walls standing – it has been lovingly restored. The central tower of the chateau collapsed recently and nowadays it is privately owned, so you can't get in, but it looks romantic enough, through the fence and across pretty parterre gardens. There are still eight pepper-pot towers left.

Daniel Thiriez is a man in his mid-thirties who, in his own way is going to put Esquelbecq on the map. In January 1997, he opened a micro-brewery and presented the village and the world with a new beer, *La Blonde d'Esquelbecq*. The tourists – French, British, Dutch and Belgian – have already started to arrive. *They* are here for the beer.

Between the wars, there were three breweries in this tiny village, but one by one, they all went out of business. It's satisfying, and appropriate, that Thiriez' new brewery should be set up on the premises of one of the old ones – his house and brew-house are in the former Brasserie Poidevin-Vandenameele, a *ferme-brasserie* which used to make beer and farm chicory. There is a faded photograph of the old establishment on the wall of the new business.

In one sense, Monsieur Thiriez is taking a courageous leap into the dark. He is from Lille and until a couple of years ago, was head of the personnel department of a large multi-national firm. He has given up the big city and the big company and opted for what he sees as a better way of life for himself, his wife and their three young children. On the other hand, he has certainly been careful – after two years of hobby home-brewing, he took himself off to college in Brussels and Nancy to learn the trade properly, and toured the small breweries of Northern France and Belgium to pick up further experience.

The Brasserie Thiriez is small, but very impressive, a brand-new sparkling ensemble of stainless steel brewing kettles, mash-tuns and fermenters, imported from Italy and set up in a spotlessly clean tiled room. Another part of the old farm has already been turned into a bar-hospitality-sales room, decked out with old agricultural and brewing machinery, posters and photographs. Make an appointment by telephone and you can view the brewery and taste the beers in some comfort. (The brewery is open from Wednesday to Saturday from 1000 – 1900).

La Blonde d'Esquelbecq is made from pale malt from French spring barley. The top fermenting yeast comes from the CERBIA laboratory in Lille – Daniel Thiriez experimented with many of them and chose this particular one because it is especially aromatic. Hops, from Poperinge, in Belgium, are Brewers' Gold, for bitterness and Saaz for aroma. The finished product is neither filtered nor pasteurised and is left to re-ferment in the bottle. It is an astonishing achievement for a first beer – golden, with a huge aromatic head, refreshing, with a nice crack of the bitter hops in the finish. It is 6.5% ABV and comes in a crown-capped 75cl bottle with an extremely neat and striking black and yellow label featuring the arms of the village and, on an additional strip running up to the cap, a picture of the *hallekerke*.

At the end of the year, Thiriez brewed his first Christmas beer, presented over a well-attended weekend of *portes-ouvertes*, to many visitors, including a flying picket from the Ghilde des Eswards Cervoisiers, who pronounced themselves highly satisfied with the new beer. La Noël d'Esquelbecq (5.8% ABV) is an amber-going-on-reddish beer, spiced with sweet and bitter orange and aniseed.

Daniel Thiriez is, I think, a happy man. The brewery seems to be doing well and he hopes to produce 600 hectolitres in 1998. His wife, Marielle Parquet, is a painter and is busy setting up a studio in another of the farm buildings. I saw one of the children, who was certainly pleased with life – he had just been presented with a prize for archery. There is a field set aside in the village for the popular local sport of *tir à la perche* which involves shooting vertically at *oiseaux*, which are small cork and feather targets, set up in ranks at the top of a thirty metre pole. Young master Thiriez had brought one down with his first shot at the beginning of the season – the trophy rested on the mantlepiece in the living room.

Les 3 Brasseurs

22 place de la Gare
5900 Lille
Tel: 03.20.06.46.25
Fax: 03.20.06.46.29

Les 3 Brasseurs stands amongst a line of busy bars and cheap hotels directly opposite the entrance to Lille-Flandres railway station. From the TGV Lille-Europe station, the Eurostar terminal, walk down the Avenue Le Corbusier to the Lille-Flanders station.

Les Trois Brasseurs, opened here in 1986 by Patrick Bonduel, was the first brewpub in France. Monsieur Bonduel's Company, Bars de France, has since introduced several more, including Les 3 Brasseurs in Angers and Strasbourg and O'Neil's in Mulhouse and Paris.

The idea of a bar/restaurant, with its own tiny brewery, was a return to basics for Patrick Bonduel. His father and grandfather had headed the Pelforth brewery in Lille, as well as holding a substantial slice of the company's shares. His father, the late Jacques Bonduel took over other breweries, after the Heineken conquest of Pelforth – they have all since closed. Patrick concentrated on the idea of the micro-brewery/restaurant, with spectacular success.

If it is a fine day, many of the customers at Les 3 Brasseurs like to sit out under the canopy at the front of the establishment, to take the air and keep an eye on the hustling goings-on in the street. The real atmosphere, however, is indoors. The narrow entrance bar takes you past the brewery itself – beyond that are several rooms of various sizes, ranging from tiny tap-room dimensions to large dining and drinking areas. It can get very busy and noisy, especially at lunch-time. If it is hectic, then the waiter service can become terse and to the point.

If it is your first time and you feel at all intimidated or confused, pick up one of the many copies of what looks like a newspaper, La Gazette, and browse, thoughtfully. In the centre-spread, surrounded by articles on the history of beer, the health-giving properties of beer brewed *sur place*, quizzes on beer and recipes for *cuisine à la bière*, there is the beer and food menu.

To test-fly the beers, the sensible thing to do is ask for a *palette*, which is a wooden tray on which are trapped three, or four, 15cl glasses, each one with a different example of the micro-brewery's production. The four-glass *palette* will provide you with the full usual repertoire of the place – a *blonde* (5.2% ABV), an *ambrée* (6.2% ABV), a *brune* (6.4% ABV) and *La Blanche de Lille* (4.6% ABV). There are seasonal brews in the spring (La Bière de Mars) and for Christmas (La Haute du Père Noël).

All the beers are top-fermented and lightly filtered, but not pasteurised. As the Gazette points out, they could hardly be fresher, since they come directly from the brewery before your very eyes. In every case, malt predominates over hop. I can do no better than to quote Roger Protz, who describes the *blonde* as having a "malty, perfumy aroma with a bitter-sweet palate", the *ambrée*, he says, has a "dark toasty character", while the *brune* has "hints of sweet nuts and bitter chocolate". (I lack Roger Protz' iron resolve and have always got carried away with the atmosphere of the place and failed to take coherent notes). The Blanche de Lille can be bought in 75cl bottles (at a stratospheric price of 35F) for home consumption – notes in the tasting section at the back.

La Gazette also offers beer cocktails – some seem bizarre in the extreme – Nord Express is the *blonde*, with cassis and lemon juice, Russian Bière is *blonde* plus vodka and lemon juice, while Zythum is a new name for an old favourite of Northern France, a *blonde* with a shot of *genièvre de Houlle* – gin.

The food is simple – either go for a *flammekeuche maison*, a pizza-based confection with a variety of toppings – or have set lunch (only from 1130 to 1430), which will be a main course *plat du jour*, chocolate mousse or crème caramel, plus coffee, at 59F. The "Welsh" (rarebit), with chips and a beer, is another standby. Next time, you will perhaps have a more relaxed trawl through the Gazette and try the *Lapin à la bière*, the *carbonade flamande*, the *maroilles affiné à la bière*, or the *tarte à la bière*.

The bar-micro-brasserie-restaurant is open every day from 1100 – 2400.

Another 3 Brasseurs opened in Lomme, on the outskirts of Lille, in early 1998:

3 Brasseurs
8 rue du Chateau d'Isinghein
59150 Lomme
Tel: 03.20.22.13.80

Off the N352 Lille north-west ring-road, at exit 5. Follow the signs for Lomme Bourg and Centre Commercial. Once off the motorway make sure you get in lane for the Centre Commercial. The 3 Brasseurs is in the middle of a new trading estate. It is a low two-storey brick and fake stone building, marked by a handsome brick chimney. Accompanying attractions on a vast site include Kinepolis (Le Chateau du Cinema), Planet Bowling, a Pizza Hut, Tex-Mex restaurant, Buffalo Grill, a couple of hotels and yes – a MacDonalds. I'm sure you get the picture.

Inside the 3 Brasseurs is a barn, but a nicely done barn, with olde-world timber posts and beams, barrels for a ceiling and complex compartmentalised seating arrangements. You can settle in the "office", with pictures of several generations of the influential Bonduel family, or on the back of a splendid old Peugeot flat-back delivery truck, among other nooks and crannies. Old photos on the walls are interesting.

Service here is fast and friendly – something of a contrast to the attention you get these days in the centre of Lille. The beers and menu are exactly the same. An interesting place to stop if you happen to be passing by. You could buy a green 3 Brasseurs apron, or samples of the beers to take away, if you felt so inclined, at the shop. Personally, I would avoid the regular rock and roll concerts.

For the record, Patrick Bonduel's other establishments (where the beers and the food and the Gazette are exactly the same) are:

Les 3 Brasseurs
Centre Commercial Les Halles
Place Mondain Chanlouineau
49100 Angers
Tel: 02.41.87.93.30

Les 3 Brasseurs
22 rue des Veaux
67000 Strasbourg
Tel: 03.88.36.12.13

O'Neil
5 place des Victoires
68100 Mulhouse
Tel: 03.89.56.25.58

O'Neil
20 rue des Canettes
75006 Paris
Tel: 01.46.33.36.66

Distillerie Claeyssens

1 rue de la Distillerie
BP16
59118 Wambrechies
Tel: 03.20.14.91.97
Fax: 03.20.14.91.99

Sharper-eyed readers may have noticed that this is a distillery, not a brewery. They have been making *genièvre* (gin) here since 1817. Wambrechies is to the north-west of Lille, signposted off the north-west ring-road. You will see the distillery to the left, just before you hit the final bend to the centre of the town.

Claeyssens have a thriving visitor policy and if you make arrangements beforehand, you can tour the place, with a guide, most of the week except Sundays. They really only cater for groups of 14 or more, so you may have to fit in with someone else's tour. There is a charge, currently 40FF, which includes a tasting of gins.

Claeyssens are included here because in late 1997, they announced that they were in the throes of experimenting with a beer – a *bière au genièvre* – called La Claeyssens. Interesting to compare this with L'Abbatiale de St-Amand, from the Brasserie des Amis-Réunis.

Interbrew
14 avenue Pierre-Brosselette
BP No 9
59426 Armentières
Tel: 03.20.48.30.30
Fax: 03.20.48.31.97

The Belgian Breweries Artois of Leuven (famous for Stella Artois) and Piedboeuf of Jupille-sur-Meuse, near Liege (best known for its Jupiler brand) merged in 1987 and acquired the name Interbrew in 1990. The French Motte-Cordonnier Brewery in Armentières had already gone into subservient partnership with the Piedboeuf company in the late 1960s. Interbrew stopped production at Armentières in 1993 and now uses the place as a conditioning, packaging and distribution centre for its Belgian beers, such as Stella Artois, Jupiler, the Abbaye de Leffe range of top-fermented abbey-style brews, Hoegaarden, La Bécasse and the rest.

There are two reasons for mentioning the brewery – one is that for many years there were hopes, never fulfilled, that Interbrew would find space in the buildings for a visitor centre and a museum of North French brewing. You never know, it may happen one day. Interbrew *do* welcome visitors – to the tune of a million a year – to their breweries in Leuven, Jupille, Hoegaarden and Belle-Vue (Brussels), all in Belgium, of course.

The other reason for this note is that there are people who like to collect, examine and photograph old breweries – and the Motte-Cordonnier plant, externally at least, is a wonderful example of extravagant post World War One reconstruction.

As of January 1998, the establishment has been officially re-named, and will now be called the Brasserie Stella Artois.

GAZETTEER

What follows is a list, regionally organised, of bars cafés, pubs, estaminets, bistros, brasseries, tavernes and restaurants in Northern France where it should be possible to sample some of the local beers. The list was compiled from recommendations by individual members of *Les Amis de la Bière* and Gambrinus France, not forgetting a handful of exiled CAMRA members. Several suggestions came from Northern French brewers and/or their representatives. I have visited most, but not all of them. As far as I know, no-one has attempted such a listing before. There are bound to be mistakes and there will certainly be omissions. I shall enjoy being put right.

The wrap-up term most frequently used in France is café. Thus, ever gloomier reports in the French national press write of 69,000 cafés closing in 1995 alone, or a decline from 200,000 cafés in 1960 to a projected 40,000 by the turn of the century. They are being killed off, as are churches, boulangeries, épiceries, boucheries and charcuteries by what the French call the *auto-frigo*-télé phenomenon – people drive to the supermarket, stock up in the fridge or freezer and stay at home watching television. Just like home, really. On a more cheerful note, Jean-Pierre Hernandez called his delightful ramble through the bars of Dunkirk, written in 1993, "Cafés Dunkerquoise". The word café came north, from Paris, where the first coffee-houses appeared at the end of the seventeenth century.

A café, then, is something more than a simple bar, where you will be able to get a drink, alcoholic or otherwise, and perhaps something to eat. The range is enormous. The best of them are humming social centres, with *babyfoot* (table football), *le flipper* (pin-ball machine) and *billard* (pool) for the younger clientele, card schools (incomprehensible, but cheerful and noisy games of *manille* or *belote*), a free newspaper or two and conversation for the older end. The café with the PMU (Pari Mutuel Urbain) – the betting shop – is the place to be, especially late Saturday or Sunday mornings, when most of the bets are made and the whole world is there. It may also have a LOTO counter, where you can lose on the National Lottery and on a host of exotic scratchcards. There will be encouraging hand-written notices telling you of the latest fantastic winnings. A wall of notices is usually devoted to the local sports club and/or football team. In a place such as this, the *patron* will be energetic, voluble, friendly and extremely hard working.

At the other end of the scale, there is the café with the surly, uncommunicative, bad-tempered owner. He tends to wear a T-shirt with sweat-stained armpits, has a cigarette permanently smouldering in his mouth and reads the paper all day. Your request for a drink will be received with barely disguised contempt. There is a deafening music from tape or radio (and pop music in France is the worst on the planet) and there are two silent and morose drinkers at the bar, staring into space and listening.

I have often heard complaints of the "unfriendliness" of French cafés. In some cases, this is true – for some reason or other, yes, it is true, the *patron* does appear to dislike almost everybody. On the other hand, I do find it odd that the people who complain of "unfriendliness" in France often speak little or no French at all and seem to think that they should be able to get by, and command affection, by speaking English very-slowly-positively-and-loudly I often wonder what would happen if a Frenchman or woman came to one or other of my locals around Oldham (Lancs) and behaved like that.

Then there is the matter of basic etiquette. A Frenchman, entering a café, will greet everyone he knows – if he doesn't know anyone, he will at least say "bonjour messieurs, mesdames" to the world at large. The entrance into the familiar ground of the regular café will be followed by handshakes all round for the men, and pecks on both cheeks for the women. Try the "bonjour", and the handshakes, although perhaps postpone the kisses until you know people a little better.

The word "brasserie" may cause initial confusion, because it means brewery, but it also signifies a café with a decent menu – fast-food in the sense of brisk service. Way back, it may well be that the brasserie was a simple restaurant with its own brewery. If the sign says "bar-café-brasserie", there will be just that – a simple bar for a drink, a café in the hinterland with snacks, and a more serious eating area further back.

No-one knows for certain exactly where the term "estaminet" came from. It's a Flemish word which spread south and at its most basic an estaminet was a café. there are enjoyable arguments as to the derivation of the word – it may be from the Germanic "stamon", which was the central post holding up a roof, or a corruption of the Dutch word "stamen", a thread from which one weaves cloth. More fanciful explanations include the Flemish "sta Mynheer" ("stay, Sir"), or the Spanish/Flemish "esta minetta" ("there are young girls here"). I mention all these possibilities because I've had each one advanced passionately as the correct derivation.

There are many loving and nostalgic descriptions of the estaminet of sixty or seventy years ago – places open all days and well into the night, providing refreshment and honest simple food, social centres for weddings, christenings and funerals, meeting places for traditional pastimes such as cock-fighting, *fléchettes* and *javelot* (vastly different variations on darts) and *boule Flamande* (the Flemish version of petanque, played with flat-sided boules) and may other games peculiar to the region. There would be a *vierpot* – a metal bowl full of hot embers, set on the table for lighting communal pipes. On one of the walls there would be a notice, with a very strange design of an eye in a triangle, surrounded by angels, saying "God Ziet Mij ... Hier Vloekt Men Niet" ("God is watching me ... No-one blasphemes here"). The "zaggerman" or "scieur" was a counterbalanced figure of a sawyer, complete with large saw – if rocked, he kept sawing for quite some time. He was set in motion by the *patron*, either to indicate drinking-up time, or to conclude a tedious argument between customers – a splendid idea.

It seemed as if the estaminet had all but vanished in the 1960s and 70s and then there was a small but significant and miraculous revival. Pioneers opened up new places, firmly based on the old pattern, usually only opened at the weekends, the notion being to recreate the good old times not just for locals, but for visitors as well. (Try the Blauwershof, at Godewaersvelde, the Vierpot, at Boeschèpe, both of them just outside Bailleul – and Het Labyrint, at Kemmel, just over the border in Belgian Flanders).

Once these places became popular and fashionable, other writers, journalists and pub-crawlers discovered that many of the old estaminets had not disappeared at all, but were still struggling gamely on, usually run by old ladies or couples who hadn't been told that they were out of date. (Look up the Café Breda, near Steenvoorde, L'Haguedorne, near Cassel, L'Etoile du Jour, in St-Sylvestre).

The "Taverne Flamande" is an estaminet (a bar), with a restaurant, specialising in Flemish dishes. You can usually drink in the estaminet without necessarily eating in the taverne.

A "pub", in the North of France, is a café with an English or an Irish – or sometimes a Welsh – theme. The English version is a mass of mock-Edwardian polished brass and wood, a theatrical glory to behold. There is a chain of franchises, scattered throughout France, called "Au Bureau", obviously based on the British pattern, although the only British beers on offer, from a large international list, are Martins Pale Ale, Douglas and what is described as New Castle (Bière dorée, mi-forte). The Irish pub, one proprietor confided, was cheaper to establish, because all you needed was a collection of suitable advertising plaques, a tape-deck full of Celtic music and the Guinness.

French friends who have visited Britain grow saucer-eyed with incomprehension when they describe opening hours – or rather closing times. There are tales – a little out of date, I tell them – of being turfed out of pubs from 3pm until 6pm, or of the desert that is Sunday. In France, hours are longer and infinitely more flexible. Although I have tried to give hours for most cafés, I have always been told that, although they may open at a specific (usually early) hour in the morning, the closing time depends on how many customers there are in the place. In the country, they might shut up shop at seven in the evening, in the larger towns, especially at the weekends, they may stay open until the early hours. So don't blame me – I'm just trying to be helpful.

For the sake of convenience, and travelling time, I have grouped the establishments into areas, using old names – Flandres, Artois, Hainault, L'Avenois and the rest – which have been reused extensively in leaflets and maps in recent years by the Nord-Pas de Calais Regional Tourist Board. (The annual Nord-Pas de Calais publication "Découverte" would be a useful supplement to this guide. It is available free in Tourist Offices everywhere, or by post before your trip, from the Regional Office in Lille – the address is in the list at the back of this book).

You should bear in mind that these territories were feudal and fragmentary, then part of Burgundian, Spanish and Austrian empires, until they were finally absorbed by France in the seventeenth and eighteenth centuries. These things matter. There were times when the northern empire struck back – which accounts for otherwise baffling references to, for example, "Spanish" influences on architecture and social customs in Northern France.

Bière de Noël

BRASSÉE EN FLANDRE

8 % vol. Alc.   BRASSERIE DE SAINT SYLVESTRE 59114   75 cl Cat S

1. FLANDERS

There are borders set up by officials and recognised by administrators – and there are less certain frontiers, of thought, custom and affection. The line which divides France from Belgium was drawn up during the Congress of Vienna, which sought to tidy up after the Revolutionary and Napoleonic Wars. (The Northern state was then called the United Provinces; it split into Holland and Belgium in 1830). Look on the map south of Poperinge and Ypres and you will see a wave of distinctly un-French sounding place names – Steenvoorde, Zegerscappel, Herzeele, Bollezeele, Wormhout, Esquelbecq – spreading down into France. Spend some time in the area and you will be aware of a repertoire of much-loved Flemish traditional games, a rash of Flemish signs and symbols and an individual *cuisine Flamande*. You may sometimes hear Flemish spoken in cafés and estaminets.

The area is marked out by Bailleul and Hondschoote along the Belgian border, by Bray-Dunes, Dunkerque and Grande-Synthe along the coast, by Hazebrouck and Steenwerck to the south. It is mostly flat, with the delightful exception of the "Monts des Flandres" – a bucolic range of miniature green hummocks around Bailleul and over the border into Belgium, with a small but startling isolated knuckle of a hill at Cassel.

When a Monsieur Colpaert, a local worthy of Bailleul, was seeking inspiration for a name for the local carnival giant, back in 1853, he chose Gargantua, Rabelais's glorious creation. Neither Gargantua nor Rabelais had anything to do with the area, but Monsieur Colpaert reasoned, the Flamands were *bon mangeurs et franc buveurs* – "hearty eaters and enthusiastic boozers" – and Gargantua would have been proud of them. He would be, and they are.

BREWERIES

Beck (Bailleul)

St-Sylvestre (St-Sylvestre-Cappel)

Thiriez (Esquelbecq)

BAILLEUL

Pleasant town, with centre entirely restored Flemish fashion after the utter devastation of the First World War. Gargantua, the town giant, rolls out on Shrove Tuesday. Permanent chip vans moored in the Grand'Place. Bailleul is billed as being in the "heart of the Monts des Flandres". The tourist office in the Grand'Place (Tel: 03.28.43.81.00), is a useful source of information and maps.

Ferme Brasserie Beck: see details in breweries section

BERGUES

Lovely little town, still hiding behind moats and complex seventeenth and eighteenth century gatehouses and fortifications. Invest in Bergues cheese; its orange-yellow rind is washed regularly in beer during the maturing process.

Le Breughel

1, rue du Marché aux Fromages
59380 Bergues

Tel: 03.28.68.19.19

Open every day, lunchtimes and evening.

Reputedly the oldest house in Bergues – come into town by the Porte de Dunkerque and you will find it by the canal side, on the left. Brilliantly daft restaurant which seeks to recreate a Breughel painting of Flemish peasantry enjoying themselves. The idea is that you should do the same. Plain trestle tables, wooden chairs, wooden plates, roaring fires and fascinating paraphernalia on the walls. The waitresses carry the sixteenth century well, but the waiters can't help looking a bit self-conscious in tights and silly hats. Simple fare, splendid portions – try the *poulet à la bière*, or *carbonade flamande.* Draught beers from St-Omer. Small but good list of Belgian bottled beers – Chimay, Duvel, Rodenbach, etc.

BOESCHEPE

A hill-top village in the Monts des Flandres. The place you are looking for is outside the village, right next door to the prominent windmill.

De Vierpot

125, rue du moulin
59299 Boeschèpe

Tel: 03.28.48.46.37

Closed Monday out of season. Opens about 1000, closes when they feel like it, but usually 2200 during the week, early hours at weekends. Big day on New Year's Day, when they celebrate until 0400 and release what they call the first French Onion Soup of the year.

Worth a long detour, especially if visited in conjunction with the Blauwershof, just down the road in Godewaersvelde. The Vierpot, run by Jean Maris, is a faithful, nicely shabby and cluttered recreation of an estaminet, in the shadow of the sails of the restored post mill, the Ondankmeulin, or Moulin de l'Ingratitude. Wander round and find a room that suits you – if you can find a seat. It can get very crowded at weekends and in the season. Occasional exhibitions of Flemish art and poetry, outbursts of folk music. A vast list of beers, almost all from Belgium – but they should have the odd Jenlain or Trois Monts. Snacks, mainly open sandwiches of paté or cheese.

BOLLEZEELE

Small village, best known for its high quality Logis de France hotel-restaurant, the Hostellerie Saint-Louis. Meanwhile, down in the Grand'Place …

Café du Centre

4, Grand'Place
59470 Bollezeele

Tel: 03.28.68.02.15

Closed Monday. Bar open 0830 "until the customers have gone". Restaurant open lunchtime and evenings.

Very much a locals' place. The bar has a stove blasting out heat in winter. Old postcards of the region on the wall. Pelforth on draught, and bottles include Trois Monts and Esquelbecq. Neat, spic and span small restaurant next door to the bar has a 65F menu du jour (80F at weekends) –

simple food, gigantic portions. Madame Annie Duhoo is justly proud of the place and very welcoming.

Further along the same terrace, at 18 Grand'Place, is the *Café de l'Hôtel de Ville*, a very quiet, absolutely plain but spotlessly clean time-warped estaminet c 1950. A very pretty ornamental stove. Small bottles of Pelforth – and that's about it.

There is a classic open pissoir behind the church in the Grand'Place.

BORRE

Borre is blasted by the busy N42 from Hazebrouck to Bailleul. It has an interesting church and:

Au Bon Accueil

Place de Borre
59190 Borre

Tel: 03.28.41.56.32

Closed Monday and Saturday lunchtime, otherwise open lunch and evenings.

A cheerful restaurant where almost all the main dishes are grilled over a raging open fire. (Make sure you sit within sight of the action, which can be spectacular, but out of

danger of being grilled yourself). Hearty and copious fare; chips with everything. A good beer list, mostly the exotica from Interbrew, but includes Trois Monts, which comes from St-Sylvestre, just up the road.

CAESTRE

Caestre is on the road from Bailleul to Cassel. Going west from Caestre, pass the turn to Steenvoorde on the right, and start looking on the left – hard, for:

Café du Commerce aux Bestiaux

787, avenue General de Gaulle
59190 Caestre

Tel: 03.28.40.16.17

Open early every day, but may close early evening.

The yellow painted sign on the brick wall has almost faded away – the only other clue is a sign for Brune Vega beer (which Jupiler stopped making years ago). Don't be put off – walk in. You are not really here for the beer, which is Pelforth in bottle only, but for the experience. Monsieur and Madame Westelynck-Ghesquiere plod on, slowly, running this ancient estaminet. There is a splendid rough but expressive painting on one wall of customers in the place in the 1930s, the "God Ziet Mij" sign, and the traditional brewers' star inset in the tiled floor. The classic small bar counter now has flowers stuck in the pump pedestal.

CASSEL

No trip to or through French Flanders would be complete without a few hours spent in Cassel. Whichever way you approach the town you will have to drive up steep, twisting roads, some of them still cobbled and a challenging test of shock absorbers and teeth fillings. The Grand Old Duke of York, who, you will remember, had ten thousand men, marched them up to the top of the hill and marched them down again – this was the Mont de Cassel and the Duke of York's totally incompetent and disastrous campaign, in the late eighteenth century, is one of those stories we don't hear much about in the annals of British military history. Cassel has been fought over for centuries, right up to the Second World War, when a detachment of the British Army was overwhelmed, trying to cover the retreat from Dunkirk in 1940.

One of the creation-myths of Mont Cassel concerns an unpleasant giant who was causing trouble in the area – eating people, and so on. To stop his depredations, the locals placed in his path a giant barrel of beer. Naturally, he stopped and drank the lot, fell over dead drunk and was finished off by the said locals. They covered him with a mound of earth – and that mound is Mont Cassel. Cassel has a couple of friendly giants, Reuze Papa and Reuze Mama. Reuze Papa comes out for the February carnival, both emerge for the big day, which is Easter Monday. The Easter frolics in Cassel are amazing. I have given up trying to understand the iconography of it all, but it involved the "dancing" giants, bands playing from dawn, a kaleidoscope of strange characters, a riot of cross-dressing and disguise, lots of carnival heads, and a float, called *le Four merveilleux*, where individual spectators are seized from the crowd, plunged into the flaming oven, and emerge completely changed at the other end. It goes without saying that a deal of beer is drunk at carnival time.

You should make a two-tier visit. Park first of all in the cobbled Grand'Place (also called the Place Général de

Gaulle). The museum is here and would normally be an early port of call. Postpone that particular visit until 2001, when it is due to be reopened after extensive and expensive refurbishment, as the Museum of Flanders. The Tourist Office, with unusually knowledgeable and helpful staff, is on the other, higher, side of the Grand'Place.

Café de la Chaumière

10, Grand'Place
50670 Cassel

Tel: 03.28.40.58.02

Open every day – although on a wet winter's day, they might give up.

Stella Artois on draught – as in apparently all the cafés in the Grand'Place – but a *cave à bières* from which the young owners might be able to find you a French bottle or two. The last truly traditional, basic and scruffy bar in Cassel. The open-air pissoir affords splendid views of the Grand'Place over the wall.

La Taverne Flamande

34, Grand'Place
59670 Cassel

Tel: 03.28.42.42.59

Closed Tuesday evening and all day Wednesday.

A straight forward, old fashioned, reasonably priced Flemish speciality restaurant, recommended by a member of *Les Amis de la Bière*.

A La Hôtel de Ville (Chez Jacky)

21, Grand'Place
59670 Cassel

Tel: 03.28.42.41.38

Open every day 0730 – 2200 in the summer. Closes 2200 in winter – and "might get a bit erratic" if the weather is bad.

Café, cheap and cheerful fast-food restaurant, with *Crêpes Flamandes (Vlaamse pannekoeken)*. Menus in French, Flemish and English. A decent list of mainly Belgian beers, but Trois Monts, Jenlain, etc, as well.

It is essential to go to the very top of the Mont de Cassel – you can walk, liver, lungs and lights permitting, up curious rustic steps, from the Grand'Place. With a car, you should continue uphill from the Grand'Place, turn right into the square at the top of the hill, past the "Garage des géants", where Reuze Papa and Reuze Mama are safely installed in between performances. Turn right again and continue climbing, hoping that there are no cars coming in the opposite direction.

You end up in a large parking area called the *Terrace du Château*. The view is sensational, with roads like ribbons unspooling arrow-straight to the horizon and there is a panel to tell you what you are looking at. Back-track down the narrow lane and there are what are often described as "English" style gardens, plus a magnificent restored windmill and an equestrian statue of Maréschal Foch. Foch had his headquarters here during crucial stages of the First World War. I am not one to hero-worship the great figures of the Great War – they killed off my great-uncle Tom, for one, as well as a few million others. But the statue is impressive.

The large dilapidated building on the Terrace houses Radio Uylenspeigel, "La Voix des Flamands de France", a Flemish language radio station, which pumps out a bizarre mix of music – rock, folk, jazz, accordions – which often spills over, with an outside tannoy, the parked cars and surrounding countryside. In winter, the disc jockey's car is often the only one here and the outdoor serenade is drowned by the howling wind. The building also houses in

one corner a terrific cafe-restaurant:

T'Kasteeltje

3, Terrace du Château
59670 Cassel

Tel: 03.28.42.48.61

Opens at 1000 every day, closes whenever. In the winter, it is certainly closed Mondays and Tuesday, sometimes other days as well.

The interior is much cosier than the exterior suggests. Very good, cheap, honest food and snacks. Draught beers are Belgian, and change from time to time. There is a hefty bottle collection, again mostly Belgian, but with some of the French favourites. The Belgian proprietor runs occasional folk music festivals.

A crisis in early 1998 – the place is closed. Let's hope things are resolved soon.

If you took the easy way up, and drove, you will already have seen:

T'Kasteelhof

8, rue Saint-Nicolas
59670 Cassel

Tel: 03.28.40.59.29

The Michelin Green Guides have a recommendation "vaut de voyage", which, loosely translated, means the whole point of the trip. I doubt if the Michelin guides even mention T'Kasteelhof, but it is tempting, for beer and local tradition-lovers, touring French Flanders, to slap that imperative label on the place. Upstairs is a small estaminet-restaurant, downstairs is the shop. *The shop is open Wednesday to Saturday 1000 – 1900. The estaminet-restaurant opens, the same days, lunchtimes and evenings. In high summer – July and August – they only close on Mondays.*

First, the restaurant. Emmanuel de Quillacq and Jean-Luc Lacante are locked solidly into the local traditions and cultures of Flanders (especially), Hainault and Artois. The menu reflects that preoccupation and you really cannot go wrong, whatever you choose. *Ask* – and you shall be given. Try *saucisson à la bière, paté à la bière, hutsepot/hochepot/hot-pot*, local cheeses – anything really. There isn't much room in the restaurant and at potentially busy times, you should book.

Downstairs, in the Maison du Pays, they sell almost all the North French beers, plus *genièvres*, hydromels, fruit juices and ciders. No wines, no champagnes, because they do not come with the territory. You can also take away regional breads, patés and cooked meats, cheeses and fruit preserves – not to mention postcards and traditional carved wooden skittles

Down at ground level, around the foot of Mont Cassel, there are two more places worth hunting for:

L'Haguedoorne

2, route de Wemaers-Cappel
59670 Hardifort

Tel: 03.28.42.47.94

Closed on Sundays, otherwise open early morning to (often) fairly early evening.

L'Haguedoorne (La Haie d'épines – The Prickly Hedge) is not in Hardifort, as the address suggests. From the Cassel-Wormhout road, turn left, towards Wemaers-Cappel. The estaminet is on the left, at the first cross-roads. It looks spruced-up-modern red brick with a Kronenbourg sign outside. Once through the door, you step back fifty years into a small, clean, bare estaminet. The proprietor, a middle-aged man invariably in woolly pullover, dispenses small bottles of beer – Pelforth, or George Killian's, and conversation in Flemish, French if you must. There is a genuine small, concentric-ringed dartboard (*fléchettes*) on the wall – a well used board by the look of it. The notice-board is worth examination. Outside, where road modernisation has created an abandoned patch perfect for road-bowling, they play *boule Flamande*.

Le Petit'Bruxelles

Route Nationale
59670 Sainte-Marie
Cappel

Tel: 03.28.42.44.64

Closed all day Monday, and Tuesday evenings.

Down the road from St-Sylvestre-Cappel to Cassel, on the left. A modern looking building, standing a little way back from the road among trees and gardens. A large high-class restaurant specialising in national and regional cooking and a certain amount of *cuisine à la bière*. Bernard and Michele Desnave have been here since 1983. Bernard takes his food – and his beer – very seriously and is a member of *Les Amis de la Bière*. In 1996, Les Amis celebrated their tenth anniversary here with great ceremony, a wonderful meal and a handsome amount of approved beer. Try the *Fricassée de Volaille à la bière de Trois Monts*, cheese from the Mont des Cats Monastery, and the *Tarte à la Casonade*, if you want to stay local. If things are not too busy, Bernard will be happy to show you around his large and immaculate kitchens, and talk about beer, especially Trois Monts. A rare treat all round, although not cheap.

DRINCHAM

Drincham is on the D11, between Cassel and Bourbourg. Coming from Cassel, take the right turn after Drincham village, signposted Bergues. Immediately, on the left, is:

Au Gallodrome

41 Loogwestraete
59380 Drincham

Tel: 03.28.29.86.00

Open Friday, Saturday, Sunday 1000-1500, 1900-2300.

Jean-Bernard Claeyssen reopened Au Gallodrome in 1997. It was a simple café, which featured cock-fighting (a gallodrome is a cock-fighting arena). Now it is a small, comfortable and interestingly decorated and cluttered estaminet (to the left), a large restaurant (in the centre) and an antiques and second-hand furniture showroom (extreme right). Food is traditional Flemish. Although the sign outside says Pelforth, Monsieur Claessyssen is keen on local French beers and always has Trois Monts and Gavroche from St-Sylvestre and La Blonde D'Esquelbecq from the Brasserie Thiriez on offer, as well as an interesting choice of Belgian Flemish beers.

Technically speaking, cock-fighting is illegal in France, but in those places in the North where it can be proved that there has been a continuous and long-standing tradition, it is tolerated. The tradition continues here, three or four times a year, in one of the back rooms.

DUNKERQUE

Dunkerque ("The church in the dunes") has a long and complex history, but as far as the modern-day British tourist is concerned, there was the miracle of Dunkirk, in 1940, when over three hundred thousand British and French troops were evacuated from the beaches between Dunkerque and Bray-Dunes. No-one would claim that Dunkerque is pretty, but give the place a little time, and its character will grow on you. Fill in a few more details of tumultuous maritime history at the magnificent *Musée portuaire*, in a former tobacco warehouse in the old docks. The town hero is Jean Bart, who was *corsair* in the second half of the seventeenth century. A corsair would be a pirate if you happened to one of his English victims; an English pirate was called a privateer and was, of course, a highly respectable person. The centre of Dunkerque is the Place Jean Bart, where there is a statue of the old hero/rogue. The *carillon* in the nearby belfry chimes out the *cantata à Jean Bart*, among its repertoire of folk tunes. The Carnival, which lasts most of February, is the high spot of the Dunkerque calendar. I'm going to make it one day, because participants tell me it makes the carnival at Cassel look like a Sunday school outing. *La Bière du Carnaval de* Dunkerque, introduced for the first time in 1998, is a top-fermented *bière de garde,* introduced by a Lille entrepreneur and brewed at the Brasserie de Blaugies, in Belgium. (See Border Hopping 2). Then there are the bars ... only three in this list, which is pitiful, since I'm certain there are many others.

L'Estaminet Flamande

6, rue des Fusilliers Marins
59140 Dunkerque

Tel: 03.28.66.98.35

*Closed Monday. Weekdays
open 1000 – 0200,
weekends 1700 – 0200.*

It used to be easy to give
directions for L'Estaminet
Flamande – down by the
old docks, near permanent
mooring of the Duchesse
Anne, a magnificent sail-
training ship. They're
filling in this part of the
docks for development
now, so the nearest
landmark is the futuristic
Communité Urbaine
offices.

A fabulous place.
Downstairs bar, with plain
wooden tables and straw-
seated chairs, a spectacular
old stove and a collection
of pub games to play –
dominoes, darts, plus an
array of Flemish specials.
Newspapers and
fascinating notice-boards.
Beers on draught are from
Les Brasseurs de Gayant
(Saint-Landelin, Blanche
Amadeus etc), bottled
beers from both sides of
Flanders. French selection
includes l'Angélus, Blonde
D'Esquelbecq, Cuvée de
Jonquilles, Pot Flamand,
Goudale and many more.
The newly opened (1997)
upstairs is a restaurant/
meeting place, more
formal, but with a
magnificent *comptoir*
rescued from an old
estaminet. Excellent, good
value food, through the
whole Flemish hearty
repertoire. Betty, the
proprietress, was a
professional photographer
and is a passionate motor-
cyclist. She organises a
Rallye des Estaminets each
year in September or
October – fifty bikers
touring the best of the
Flemish estaminets and
the hop fields in a day,
quite a thought.

Aux 40 Biéres

66, rue des Forts
59210 Coudekerque-
Branche

Tel: 03.28.64.98.36

*Closed Sunday afternoons.
Opens early.*

Who could resist a café
with such a positive name.
Hard to find – off the
D916 from Bergues
towards Dunkerque. The
road runs side by side with
the canal. Turn right and
cross the canal by a green
bridge, leading to
Coudekerque-Branche.
First left over the canal.
This is an absolutely
typical café-tabac-presse –
a simple bar, newspaper
and tobacconist's shop.
The locals will be
surprised to see you.
Terken beers on draught,
with the new stout

prominent. A large floor-to-ceiling chiller cabinet has a comprehensive collection of French and Belgian beers, plus Guinness. I counted 35 beers not 40 altogether, but let it pass.

Le Pub McEwans

33, Digue de Mer
59240 Dunkerque (Malo-les-Bains)

Tel: 03.28.63.21.74

Closed Tuesday out of season, otherwise open every day, from 1100.

The "digue de mer" is the promenade, overlooking the immaculately kept beach – at weekends, the whole world is here, strolling, cycling, walking the dog, taking the air, pushing prams, hurtling along on skate-boards or roller-blades. Next to the prom, is the road, which is one-way from Dunkerque. On the other side of the road, an endless procession of snack bars, restaurants and cafés; behind them, rows of tall holiday houses, some of them quite old, with Flemish gables, decorations of coloured tile, ornate balconies and names like Mon Désir and Quo Vadis. (How did they survive 1940?) In the middle of all this is Le Pub McEwans, which doesn't look much from the

outside, but is nicely done inside, with brick walls, a barrelled ceiling, tile floors and comfortable semi-circular benched seating. Draught beers are all Interbrew, plus McEwans Scotch Ale. (The McEwans connection will be explained later, in the Lille section of the gazetteer). Around 40 bottles on the list, including Trois Monts, Jenlain, Ch'Ti.

EECKE

Eecke is a small village on the D947, between Caestre and Steenvoorde, modestly famous for its wooden *klokhuis*, or bell-tower.

Le Saint-Georges

5, rue de Caestre
59114 Eecke

Tel: 03.28.40.13.71

Open Friday and Saturday evenings 1900 – 2400. Sunday 1230 – 1530, 1900 – 2230

A homely, lively restaurant, in an old brewery building on the main road. Very popular, best to book. Eecke means an oak tree, in Flemish (It's *chêne* in French). St Wulmar founded his church here, by an old oak tree. Joelle and Dominique Tocci started their restaurant here in 1993 and the oak theme continues – they grill over a fire of oak chips and their house beer is called *La bière des chênes* (It is St-Sylvestre's Bière Nouvelle, relabelled). The food is terrific and very good value. A good beer list, French and Belgian – and you can buy some of them to take away.

GODEWAERSVELDE

In France, but, as the name suggests, a Flemish village ("Gode", for short, to its friends). Nearby is the Cistercian abbey of St-Marie-du-Mont, on top of the Mont des Cats – the Mont has an enormous television and radio mast on its summit and is the major French-Flandres landmark for passengers on the Eurostar train as it bullets from Calais to Lille. The monastery is justly famous for its cheese.

Het Blauwershof

9, Rue d'Eecke
59270 Godewaersvelde

Tel: 03.28.49.45.11

The Blauwershof (The smuggler's house) is on the south side of the village, on the D139 towards Eecke. *Open every day from 1130 onwards.* This was the first of the

revivalist estaminets on the French side of the border, opened in 1990 – many would argue, and I would not disagree, that it is still the best.

Christian Mercier presides, invariably sporting braces over a black T-shirt with the Lion of Flanders on his ample chest and generous gut. He has a fierce black moustache, beard and pony-tail as well and it is difficult to believe that he was once the chief accountant in a major bank.

The Blauwershof is a rambling, multi-roomed establishment, every room stuffed with traditional games. Try *le jeu de grenouille* (throwing discs at a complex cabinet with an assortment of targets, including a brass frog with gaping mouth), or *Billard St-Nicolas* (blow-billiards), or *421* (a dice game). Every single time I have been there, the clientele has been different, which must tell you something about the appeal of the place. Once, I ended up leaning against the bar, being fuelled by the various explanations of the word 'estaminet' by a quartet of local farmers who only spoke French because they realised I was English and couldn't cope with their Flemish. On another visit, on a Sunday, the place was packed with families on tour and eating. I was there with a group of CAMRA members who were delving rigorously into the vast collection of French, Breton and Belgian beers on offer; I was there for a *combat de coqs*, a day of cock-fighting, when the place was heaving with Belgian and French *coqueleurs* with their birds, their wives and their children. I have not yet attended a meeting of the *Guilde des Arbaletriers* (the crossbow club), or managed to get to the annual October beer-tasting session with *Les Amis de la Bière*. It is that sort of place. Cheek by jowl with the Blauwershof is:

Au Roi de pot'je vleesch

31, rue du Mont des Cats
59270 Godewaersvelde

Tel: 03.28.42.52.56

Closed Monday. They also shut up shop for a couple of weeks in October.
Georgette and Claude Duverlie run this down to earth *boucherie/charcuterie/épicerie/restaurant*, in a building that was once their simple butcher's shop, with abattoir at the back. The Duverlie's have adapted quite brilliantly to modern times and tastes. *Pot'je vleesch*, a classic Flemish dish, is a terrine of cold cooked rabbit, chicken and veal, herbs and white wine, set in gelatine. Claude is the "le Roi" – the King, of *pot'je vleesch* and you should try it here, then buy a jar to take home. The shop stocks other tempting charcuterie, plus local butter, honey and cheeses, including the *fromage des Mont des Cats*. Next door, the grocery section has local vegetables and an excellent selection of local beers, including Henri le Douanier (Trois Monts with another label). Henri is the latest of the village giants, fashioned after a nineteenth century customs officer. Smuggling has been a way of life on and over the border ever since the frontier was drawn up in the first place. There are plans for yet another giant, this time a *fraudeur*, or smuggler.

The restaurant, in the former abattoir, is a plain and simple place, excellent value. Go through the shop. I am not fond of the music, which is Flemish folky but sounds like Jimmy Shand.

HAZEBROUCK

A difficult place to get in and out of. Don't come on Monday, market day, when the Grand'Place is packed with stalls and parking is almost impossible. In any case, the Taverne is closed on Mondays …

La Taverne

61, Grand'Place
59190 Hazebrouck

Tel: 03.28.41.63.09

Closed all day Monday and Sunday evenings.

The Grand'Place is huge – La Taverne is on the opposite side of the square to the Hôtel de Ville.

One long narrow high-ceilinged room, immaculate decor, with wooden panelling and mirrors, brown leather-backed seats. Bernard Dententer runs a very tight ship and doesn't like people to hang around the bar. Buy the drinks and move to one of the tables near the entrance, or go into the restaurant further back and enjoy an interesting meal. At lunchtimes, the whole place becomes a restaurant.

There is a simple 90F menu du jour, which changes every week according to the season and what is available from the market. Saturday evening and Sunday lunch is up-market, but still good value at 145F. Try *L'Entrecôte à la Gueuze, Le contre-filet à la Kriek, Les rognons de veau flambés*

au genièvre. Friday evening from September to April is *moules-frites* night.

A riot of Flemish games to play, including *jeu de fer* (a combination of billiards and shuffleboard), *table à toupie* (miniature skittles) and *jeu de puces* (Flemish form of tiddleywinks). Belgian beers from Interbrew on draught, and a good beer list, including Trois Monts.

HERZEELE

A small village, with lovely freshly painted and polished Flemish cottages, on the country road between Wormhout (in France) and Watou (in Belgium).

Café des Orgues

Rue de la gare
59470 Herzeele

Tel: 03.28.27.63.02

The only day to go is Sunday, when they have old-time dancing from 1600 to midnight in a huge room walled by no less than three absolutely magnificent ancient fairground organs. (Only one of these monsters is played at a time). The bar outside has no draught beer, but a very good selection of Belgian bottles – and table football in the unlikely event of your ever being bored.

HONDSCHOOTE

Hondschoote is right by the border, east of Bergues, south of Bray-Dunes. The battle of Hondschoote, in 1793, raised the siege of Dunkerque, threw back the Allied armies and saved the Revolution – it is commemorated by the newly restored windmill (a focus of the battle) on the outskirts of the town, and the memorial in the Grand'Place. The bandstand (*kiosk à musique*) is pretty good too.

L'Haezepoel

3451 Chemin de l'Haezepoel
Beveren Houk
59122 Hondschoote

Tel: 03.28.62.50.50

L'Haezepoel – "hare-mere" would be a rough translation – is a restaurant *open every day except Tuesday in the summer, Thursday to Sunday in winter*. It comes highly recommended by a member of *Les Amis de la Bière*, who warns that it is in the middle of nowhere – and essential to book in summer weekends. Take the road from Steenvoorde towards Hondschoote.

After the crossroads called *les 5 Chemins*, look for the signs to the right – and keep following them for several kilometres. Mary Beudin and her mother run the place – they specialise in grills and *pot'je vleesch* and they know all about the beers from St-Sylvestre and one or two neighbouring Belgian breweries.

MORBECQUE

Morbecque is south of Hazebrouck. Once in the village, as you see the church on the left, turn right following the sign towards Wallon-Cappel. At the roadside chapel in 300m, turn left, past the cemetery. Turn right into the Rue de Romerain, then follow this road until you are almost ready to give up. The place you want is a neat building, with steep-pitched, orange-tiled roof and brown shutters, on the left, just as the road swings right towards Sercus.

A la Rue de Sercus

(Chez Jacqueline)
59190 Morbecque

Chez Jacqueline features on the front cover of Jacques Messiant's magnificent book "Estaminets des Pays du Nord". The place is universally acknowledged as the most authentic and unspoiled of all the old-generation estaminets. Jacqueline has been here for well over fifty years – when I asked her if she had many English visitors, she mentioned a parachutist who had dropped in in 1944. (They hid him in the woods and he got away and reappeared to say thank you fifty years later). The place is beautiful, but basic – expect only Pelforth bottled beers. There's a small shop here as well.

QUAEDYPRE

Quaedypre is a few kilometres south of Bergues, best approached from the D916 Bergues to Wormhout road. The village has a magnificent early seventeenth century church.

La Taverne du Westhoek

2 route de Wylder
59380 Quaedypre

Tel: 03.28.68.68.14

Open all day Thursday and Friday, Saturday evening and Sunday lunchtime.

Go straight into the village from the main road, passing the factory, the church, the school and the marie on the left. Turn right, and the Taverne is on the corner. There is a small parking area 100m beyond the place.

The Taverne opened in May 1996, on the premises of an old estaminet. Pierre and Thérèse Vandromme have a splendid place here. Outside, it is a pleasing mix of old yellow and red brick, with blue shutters and orange-tiled roof. Inside, a charmingly brac-a-brac-decorated but comfortable lounge/games room to the right, a functional small bar straight ahead and a pleasant folksy restaurant to the left. Beers include bottles of 3 Monts and Esquelbecq, draught Stella and Abbaye de Leffe. Madam Vandromme's cooking is excellent and the menu is text-book Flemish. Best to book if you want a meal. The Vandromme's change their opening days from time to time – the aim is to keep the place cheerful and full over the weekend.

SAINT-SYLVESTRE-CAPPEL

Etoile du Jour

13 Place de l'Eglise
59114 St-Sylvestre-Cappel

Tel: 03.28.40.12.74

Another time-warp estaminet, in the square behind the church and just across the road from the Saint-Sylvestre brewery.

Denise Jeffries opens every day at 0730 and closes at 2030, just as she has since she moved in here, in 1949. (She visits children and grandchildren and great-granchildren over Christmas, so the place is closed, briefly). Her late husband's father, Jack Jeffries, was a British soldier, hence the anglicised name.

L'Etoile is a spotless, polished, quiet, homely one room café with wooden bench seating, a fine stove and lots of pot plants. Postcards from friends and visitors, French, Belgian and English, on the wall. Madame Jeffries emerges from her kitchen to serve customers. The draught beers are the usual Stella/Kronenbourg assortment, but she has the full range of St-Sylvestre beers in bottle.

STEENVOORDE

Steenvoorde is a vibrant center of Flemish culture, although you might not realise this, since it is deathly quiet most of the time. No matter how quiet things are, you can always enjoy the local architecture – decorative brick and tile-work on local houses, three restored windmills within close range of the village. Arrive here on one of the village's celebratory periods, such a the Fête de

Houblon, during the first weekend in October, and you will be treated to processions featuring the village giant, Jean le Boucheron.

Café Bréda

24 Route d'Eecke
59114 Terdeghem

The address says Terdeghem, but the place is found on the Eecke road out of Steenvoorde. Leaving Steenvoorde, look out for practically the last building on the right before open country.

The Café Bréda is on the corner of the Route d'Eecke and the Route Saint-Jean – it looks like a chapel, as indeed it once was. You might spot the ancient Bières Doboës and Vega Pils signs, or the new Duvel notice. Unless the veterans are playing *boule Flamande* on the pitch outside (on warm Saturdays or Sunday afternoons), the place will look deserted and closed. In fact, the Café Bréda, also known as the Trois Moineaux or the Drie Meuches, is open every day. Monsieur et Madame Huyghe have been here since the 1940s and not much has changed since they moved in. Drink a quiet bottle of Duvel, or Pelforth, try a gentle game of *fléchettes* or *peule pek* (they call this "pitchin' in t'pot" in Lancashire, where I come from), read the local paper, chat to the *patron*. It can't last long, so enjoy it while you can.

Auberge de Noordmeulen

Route de Wormhout
59114 Steenvoorde

Tel: 03.28.48.11.18

The Noordmeulin, or Moulin du Nord, restored in the late 1970s, is one of Steenvoord's three windmills. In the shadow of the mill is the Auberge de Noordmeulen, a Flemish restaurant highly recommended by members of *Les Amis de la Bière*. There is a set menu at a very reasonable 108F and there are dishes cooked in beer – *carbonade* and *lapin à la bière brune*. They sell goat cheese as well. You have to book.

La Taverne

14 Grand'Place
59114 Steenvoorde

Tel: 03.28.48.16.32

Closed on Mondays. Open 0900 – 2400.
One long room, extremely neat, clean and comfortable. Madame Mylene Plouviez seems to spend her time polishing when she is not working at the bar. Stacked with football trophies, so there is a lot of polishing to be done. Splendid jukebox, plus electronic darts, pool, table football. Immaculate posters on the wall include Johnny Hallyday, Bob Marley and AC/DC – an eclectic mix. Thirty sorts of beer, although the most interesting ones, from France and Belgium, are in bottle.

STEENWERCK

Steenwerck is a few kilometres south-east of Bailleul; it is a pleasant village slowly being swamped by modern development. Find the church, then follow the signs to the museum.

A la Gaieté

Musée de la vie rurale
59181 Steenwerck

Tel: 03.28.49.9.78

Open only on Sunday afternoons, from 1500 to 1900. (They stop serving at the bar at 1830).

A La Gaieté is a "traditional" estaminet within the Museum of Rural Life. It is a wonderful place, staffed by very friendly volunteers and it is usually full of customers enjoying themselves. A whole room full of traditional games, all of which can be played; there is an original *billard Rousse* table – this is a rare example of the game which inspired an English entrepreneur in the 1930s to develop bar-billiards. The bar is good too, with a comprehensive selection of Northern French beers, sold by the bottle or the glass. Not to be missed – but be careful of those limited opening hours.

WATTEN

Watten is a pleasant village by the canalised River Aa, north of St-Omer. You can watch the barges go by, climb Mount Watten, the very last of the Flanders "mountains", to look over the restored windmill and enjoy the splendid view. There is a Taverne Flamande in the village, but the one you want is some way away and difficult to find.

La Taverne Flamande

59143 Millam

Tel: 03.28.68.05.72

In winter, open weekends only – Friday, Saturday, Sunday. From 1 April to 1 October, closed Wednesdays.

The Taverne is on a narrow unclassified country lane. From Millam, north of Watten, take the Route de Merckenghem. The Taverne is on the right – you will see signs for Pelforth and a camp site.

Alternatively, take the road from Mont Watten towards Bollezeele (D226). Go past the road to Millam and take the next left, just before you reach the Chapelle Ste-Mildrède in the fields to your right. The Taverne is on the left. It all sounds very difficult, but dozens of British visitors find their way to the camp site, for a pre or post ferry overnight stop.

The camp site actually pre-dates the Taverne, which was a private house until 1991. Much of the old private interior has been retained – there are some magnificent eighteenth century paintings on wooden panelling, one of them a sea battle (the troublesome British again), another the view of the church which you can still see from the window of the house. The Taverne is primarily a restaurant, with a simple menu of hearty grills – beef, lamb, pork – done over an open fire inside a fireplace built in 1768. You can, if you wish, just call in for a drink. The bar has a good selection of beers, mostly Belgian, but including 3 Monts, Gavroche, Grain d'Orge and Goudale. There are huge celebrations here for the Fête du Feu de Saint-Jean in June and the Fête de la Taverne, in August.

HOPS AND
THE HOPFIELDS

Hops were known and grown and used in the production of beer in Flanders long before they arrived in England in the sixteenth century. They gradually replaced a plethora of plants, herbs and spices – yarrow, cumin, marjoram, aniseed, rosemary, juniper and others – collectively known as "gruits" – which helped to counter the natural sweetness of beer, to preserve it and to add flavouring. The *cervoise*, or *korma* of old Gaul became known as *bière* when hops replaced these earlier ingredients. Jean Sans Peur, Duke of Burgundy (which included Flanders) from 1404 to 1419, handed out medals to the best growers of hops and instituted an order of chivalry called *L'Ordre de Houblon*. (The *Chevaliers du houblon d'or*, created in 1964, is a sort of modern recreation. They are a secretive organisation, who present the *bières de mars* each year).

Flemish weavers who came to work in Kent at the beginning of the sixteenth century brought several varieties of hops with them, although it was not until the middle of the century that the plant was finally and officially accepted in Britain.

Travel the hop fields of Flanders today and you may be surprised to find a strong English influence – the tide has turned the other way and at various stages, right up to comparatively recent times, famous English (and Kentish) varieties have been adopted and names like Brewers' Gold, Northern Brewer, Challenger, Magnum, Target and Yeoman are common. (These last two, Yeoman and Target, originally developed at Wye College in Kent, were only used for the first time in France in the late 1980s, after a trial period in an experimental hop farm at Météren).

The hop fields are most apparent – giant poles and complex systems of wiring, gradually clothed and curtained in green snakes of hop – if you drive between Poperinge, in Belgium, and Steenvoorde, in France. The best time to make the trip and pay your respects is from late June, when spectacular growth begins, to late August, harvest time. Sometime in early August, local growers organise a *Journée du Houblon*, when, for a small charge, you can visit the fields and talk to growers in Bailleul, Steenvoorde, Boeschèpe and Météren, a couple of weeks before the harvest. (Contact the Tourist Office in Bailleul for details – Tel: 03.28.43.81.00). Around about the last weekend in August, Denys Beck invites visitors to actually help with his harvest in the fields around the Ferme-Brasserie Beck. The *Fête du Houblon* at Steenvoorde during the first weekend in October presents a *concours* – a presentation and judging of the first of the crop – followed by celebrations and processions in the village.

In spite of all this activity, these are difficult times for the farmers who still grow hops in French Flanders. Unsubstantiated statistics talk of 2200 hectares under cultivation before the First World War – even the experts doubt this. Recent studies show that there were almost 350 hectares in 1973, tended by 80 growers. This has fallen to 40 hectares today, with only a handful of producers. Across the border, cultivation in Belgian Flanders has dropped to somewhere between 200 and 300 hectares.

The formation of *Les Excellences Nord-Pas de Calais* in 1991 may help. To gain their coveted label, brewers have to use at least 50% regional ingredients, including hops from French Flanders. Denys Beck is grateful, but nevertheless pessimistic about the future. Micro-breweries take micro-amounts of hops. "Before long", he says, "we might find ourselves growing for a handful of breweries – and for the tourists".

Nostalgic tourists may enjoy the Musée Jeanne Devos, in Wormhout. Jeanne Devos, who died in 1989 at the ripe old age of 87, was an enormously talented photographer of everyday life in Flanders. Among the thousands of prints scattered casually on the walls and in albums in the homely museum are dozens of classic images of the hop harvests in French Flanders, which she took during the 1950s and 60s, when extra workers and their families were drafted in to cope with the labour. It all seems a long time ago. (The Musée Jeanne Devos is in the Rue de l'Eglise, and is open every day except Wednesday, from 0930 to 1200 and 1400 to 1700).

BORDER HOPPING 1

The paraphernalia of border control is now just so much diplomatic and administrative archaeology. Occasionally, when there is a terrorist scare in Paris, or a drugs chase, officers appear at the main checkpoints – the sentry boxes on minor roads remain uninhabited. If you are exploring French Flanders, then you should consider straying, totally unhindered, across the border from time to time, especially into the area around Poperinge known, delightfully and tellingly, as Hoppeland. The most comprehensive guides to beers and bars in Belgian Flanders (including Peter Crombecq's magnificent biannual Bier Jarrboek) are in Flemish. The best English language guide is Tromp's Beer Traveller in West Flanders. The only minor problem seems to be knowing what language to use – many Belgian Flemings prefer you to use English, rather than French.

Poperinge's Tourist Office, in the basement of the town hall in the main square, is a good starting point for maps, leaflets and information. (*Dienst Tourisme, Stadhuis, Grote Markt 1, 8970 Poperinge. Tel: 057.33.40.81. Fax: 057.33.75.81*) Poperinge was a rest and recreation centre for British troops pulled back from or about to be pulled into the dreaded Ypres salient, one of the killing-grounds of the First World War. Those men who chose the Christian option on salvation and sanity, rather than the bars and the brothels of the town, took refuge in Talbot House, run by the Reverend Philip Byard "Tubby" Clayton. The International Toc H movement began here. The house, on the Gasthuistraat, is still a Toc H centre and open to the public. A visit to the attic chapel, with its simple wooden carpenter's bench altar will stop you in your tracks and make you weep, Christian or no. The same can be said of the museum, recently opened just by the tourist office, to the hapless and helpless men sentenced to be shot for "cowardice" or desertion – the museum is actually the condemned cell and still has despairing graffiti on the walls.

Take a deep breath of fresh air, shake your head, and set out with one of the Poperinge leaflets – the *Plokkersroute* – the hop-pickers' road; the *Route des Monts de Flandre Sans Frontières* (which includes the Blauwershof in Godewaersvelde and the Vierpot in Boeschèpe on the French side of the border); the *Hoppeland Route*, or the interesting Traditional Games route, for which you pay a fee of 650BF and get fed and watered and taught half a dozen undemanding Flemish games during the course of a self-propelled wander around splendid old estaminets and bars.

The National Hop Museum, also in the Gasthuistraat, is well worth a visit, although opening hours can be tricky – it is open every afternoon from 1400-1700 in July and August, Sunday afternoons only in May, June and September. Celebrations of the hop seem to get more popular as the actual industry declines. There is a National Beer Weekend every year, during the third weekend in September. Every three years, this is extended into the famous Hop Festival, Procession and Pageant (the next one is 1999).

If you want to stay in Poperinge, then you can do no better than book into the Hotel Palace. (*Ieperstraat 34, 8970 Poperinge. Tel: 057.33.30.93. Fax: 057.33.35.35*) Guy and Beatrijs Osteux-Beernaert are absolutely charming hosts. The Palace has a bar with a wonderful selection of Belgian beers and a very good restaurant. There is an annual Belgian Beer Festival here, held over the August Bank Holiday weekend. CAMRA members are offered a

10% discount on room prices – take your membership card.

There are several breweries within striking distance of Poperinge and the border. Among the most interesting are the St Sixtus Abdij, a Trappist Monastery with a drive-in beer bay. You have to buy by the twenty four bottle case and there is money back on the empties. Regulars have the whole operation down to a fine art. The bottles are unlabelled, but strength is indicated by different coloured crown caps. If the monastery is closed, the Café In de Vrede, across the road, sells the beers as well. (*St Sixtus Abdij, Donkerstraat 12, 8640 Westvleteren. Tel: 057.40.10.57*)

The Brouwerij Café d'Hellekapelle sells a fierce and delicious range of beers brewed by Stef Orbie in a shed on the other side of the car park. The café is in deep countryside off the Watou to Abeel road. It is open weekend afternoons (Friday, Saturday and Sunday) and evenings. (*Stoppelweg 26, 8978 Watou. Tel: 057.38.86.66*)

Watou has two breweries, one of which, the Brouwerij Van Eecke, you can visit by making arrangements and paying a small fee at the tourist office in Poperinge. The brewery's Poperings Hommelbier is justly famous. The other Watou brewery makes St-Sixtus Abbey beers under licence, which is very confusing, since they appear to be quite different to the existing Abdij St Sixtus beers. In Watou's main square, you will find t'Hommelhof, a high-class restaurant specialising in *cuisine à la bière*. (*t'Hommelhof, 17 Watouplein, 8978 Watou. Tel: 057.38.80.24. Fax: 057.38.85.90*)

Noel Cuvelier is getting to be a famous figure for adventurous cross-channel shoppers. Noel runs a beer shop – he also sells chocolates, cheeses, souvenirs, groceries, dog food, calor gas and lots of other things. Coming from Steenvoorde to Poperinge, five minutes after you have crossed the border, you will see Noel's farm, set back of the road to the left. It is signposted, but you will probably spot the flags flying in his farmyard first. Noel speaks all languages and is a whiz with his calculator, working out exchange rates in the blink of an eye – he seems to accept almost any currency. The beer collection is dazzling. (You can get much better chocolates, though, at the Maison de Praline, just up the road). (*Cuvelier's Beer Shop, Abelestationsplein 30, 8970 Watou. Tel: 057.33.33.05. Open every day, 0800 – 2000*)

Finally, if you enjoyed the Blauwershof or the Vierpot, or any of the revivalist estaminets in France, then you should make an effort to visit Het Labryrint, at Kemmel, in the Heuvelland, south of Ypres. (The village is north of Mont Kemmel, another of the Monts des Flandres). Stéphane Dehollander has some claim to be the pioneer of this sort of thing – he restored an old estaminet, and its *boule* pitch, at Dranouter, back in 1973, then moved to Wulvergem and did the same thing, very successfully, all over again. Het Labyrint, on a corner of the village green in Kemmel, has a bar generously stocked with Belgian beers and tables full of Flemish games, a restaurant and function room, a museum of traditional games, a museum of local Celtic history and an art gallery, all piled up three floors. The whole place is littered with astounding displays of bric-a-brac, sacred and profane. Outside, there is a hedge-maze (hence Het Labyrint) and another assortment of games. (*Het Labyrint, Dries 29, 8956 Kemmel. Tel: 057.44.65.81. Closed Tuesday*)

2 COAST TO COAL

Coast to Coal is a fanciful way of corralling an area which runs from the coast below Flanders, including Gravelines, Calais, Boulogne, Berck-sur-Mer and their hinterlands, then runs inland to include St-Omer, Aire-sur-la-Lys, Etaples, Montreuil and Hesdin. In French territorial terms, it encompasses the *Calaisais*, the *Boulonais*, the *Audomarois*, the *Canche-Athie* and the *Sept Valleés*. The territory peters out at St-Pol-sur-Ternoise and Lillers – the latter on the western edge of the *Bassin Minier*.

Breweries

Le Moulin à Bière, Coquelles

St-Omer

St-Poloise, St-Pol-sur-Ternoise

Café de la Poste, St-Pol-sur-Ternoise

BERCK-PLAGE

Vast, old-established and curiously old-fashioned seaside holiday resort, with sand strewn streets laid out in ruler straight lines. Amusement arcades, a casino and horse racing in summer. Sand-yacht racing and kite-flying on the fine beach. The museum has a nice collection of lesser-known Impressionist and after painters. The Bagatelle Amusement Park, extremely popular with French families, is not far away.

Le Voltaire

29 avenue Général de Gaulle
62600 Berck-Plage

Tel: 03.21.84.43.13

Out of season, open 1100 – 0100 (Fri, Sat to 0200), closed Tuesday. During the season open every day 0900 – 0200.

It is easy to get lost and desperate in Berck. The Voltaire is 200m from the sea, very close to the Casino – follow signs to the Kursaal.

The brothers Delannoy

109

work very hard at their café-bar-restaurant-hotel. The bar is small and modern and serves draught Jenlain and Sebourg during the season, from the bottle in winter. Belgian beers also, including classics such as Duvel and Bush. There is a snack bar – "British sandwishes" – and a neat and cosy small restaurant, where you can try *moules à la Jenlain, andouillettes à la bière* and *Le Welsh* (rarebit) with Jenlain. There are 16 rooms in the hotel, at 110-220F a night. Irish (Guinness and music) nights from time to time.

BOULOGNE-SUR-MER

Driving into Boulogne, navigating the one-way streets and finding somewhere to park can be a nerve-shredding exercise. Once the red haze disappears from the eyes, though, it is a lively, friendly and fascinating place. The old town up on high behind its towers and walls shelters the imitation St-Paul's cathedral (the basilique Nôtre Dame) and the Château-Musée. Down-town, by the docks on the river estuary, life can get frantic – but it is fun. "The Wall Street of fish", the French call it – Boulogne is France's largest fishing port.

Nausicaa, on the promenade and close to the beach, is billed as the *centre national de la mer*. For some reason, British travel writers are invariably sniffy about it – making fun of the name, bridling at its slickness and modernity. Take no notice, pay your money and learn all there is to learn about the sea. It is essential to visit Philippe Oliver's cheese shop in the Rue Thiers, where, with the help of the enthusiastic staff, you will learn all there is to learn about cheese. (see inset).

Just outside Boulogne, to the north, on the road to Wimereux, is *La colonne de la Grande armée*, which commemorates the Napoleonic army which was going to invade England in 1804. They didn't make it, of course, and the English counter-invasion of Boulogne has continued unabated from the mid-nineteenth century to the present day.

Chez Alfred

25 place Dalton
62200 Boulogne-sur-Mer

Tel: 03.21.31.53.16

Open every day 1100 – 2200. Closed 21 December – 21 January.

The Place Dalton is off the Grande Rue, on the way up to the old town. There is the Welsh Pub nearby and an Irish pub in an alleyway down to one side. Chez Alfred is a restaurant, basically one high ceilinged room (although there is another room upstairs for overflow business). Walls covered in fishnets and fish identification posters, plus a huge old photograph of the place c1937, when it first opened. A large poster of the Gladiators – how did *that* get in here? A variety of menus, from the cheap *Formule Alfred* at 89F to the *Grand Plateau Fruits de Mer*, at 380F for two people. Fish and shellfish predominate. Stella on draught, but Chi'Ti and other French beers on offer in bottle. Local *genièvres* (gins) as well.

Le Bar Hamiot

1, rue Faidherbe
62200 Boulogne-sur-Mer

Tel: 03.21.31.44.20

Open early until late, every day.

The Bar Hamiot is down by the riverside, almost opposite the tourist office. Take care crossing the road.

Quite simply, the nerve-centre of Boulogne.

The place is always busy, with fishermen at dawn, businessmen in the afternoon, night-birds until the early hours. Sporadic tourist invasions all day. Waiters in long aprons buzz about in perpetual motion. You can eat here, everything from a snack to a substantial meal. St-Omer beers on draught, plus Draught Bass. Bottles from everywhere.

Jekyll and Hyde

Rue l'Amirel-Bruix
62200 Boulogne-sur-Mer

Tel: 03.21.33.86.55

Closed Sunday. During the week, open 1200 – 0100, on Friday, Saturday and Sunday 1200 – 0200.

On the angle of the Rue l'Amirel-Bruix and the Rue Pont-de-Service, in a concrete jungle just around the corner from the bus station.

A blood-thirstily-themed bar, draped in black, decorated with skeletons, mummies in coffins and hanging men. Recent murder in the toilet, with bloodstains and sound effects. Altogether a cheerful place. At least there is Jenlain and Sebourg on draught – and a cosy little Victorian enclave built around a piano. Darts, British-style, in the back room.

Vole Hole

52 rue de Lille
62200 Boulogne-sur-Mer

Tel: 03.21.92.15.15

Open Monday 1800 – 0100, otherwise open every day 1130 – 0100.

The Vole Hole must have some claim to be the smallest bar in Europe. Twenty customers constitute a full house. It is tucked away in a pedestrianised street, almost underneath the *basilique* up in the old town. As the name suggests, it is English-owned.

The Vole Hole is a wine bar – Roger Young, who runs the place with his partner, Pamela Cook, was a wine merchant in Boulogne, until he opened this place in 1994. He has recently discovered the charms of regional beers, and now sells Angelus, from the Brasserie d'Annouellin, on draught. Others are promised, when he gets round to visiting the breweries.

CALAIS

Calais seems to have *all* the ferries. British Customs and Excise and the Brewers and Licensed Retailers Association have calculated that 1.4 million pints of beer are brought from Calais to Dover every *day*. This largely bootleg trade exists because the duty differential on beer between France and Britain is somewhere in the region of 1:6. A pint of beer at 5% ABV carries duty at 5 pence in France, 32 pence in Britain. Most of Calais seems to be devoted to supplying the British with what they desperately want – tidal waves of cheap lagers from the multinationals at low prices. Makes you weep.

The place is, of course, because of all those ferries (and the Tunnel just down the road), the main invasion point for British tourists on their way elsewhere in France, so it is perpetually clogged with traffic, most of which is not certain which side of the road it should be on.

I have to declare a disinterest here – try as one may, it is hard to like Calais. There *are* oases of calm – the Hôtel de Ville, with its belfry, and the famous Rodin statue, the *Bourgeois de Calais*, with the Parc St-Pierre opposite, the restaurant Le Channel, on the Boulevard de la Resistance. On the whole though, best to get out – quickly.

Bar à Vins

52 Place d'Armes
62100 Calais

Tel: 03.21.96.96.31

Closed Mondays.

A homely spot in the otherwise bleak and depressing Place d'Armes, where British shoppers prowl. A friendly bar and wine shop. If it is wine you want, then this is the most civilised place to buy it. They have the range of Ch'Ti beers from the Brasserie Castelain.

Moulin à Bière

(See brewery section). Once you are in the Cité de l'Europe complex at Coquelles, you might like to have a look at *Le Grenier de la Côte Opal* (closed Mondays), a couple of minutes away from the Moulin à Bière. Le Grenier sells a beautifully presented range of local and regional produce, including cheese, butter, paté, bread and jars of *rillettes de lapin, terrine de canard* and *pot'jevlesch*. They also stock a handsome collection of regional beers and badged glasses. Unfortunately, the beers tend to be over-priced. If you know what you are looking for, it is probably better to go into the *Carrefour* supermarket here and head for the regional beer section – the selection is very good, although not as comprehensive as the Grenier, but they often have spectacular price reductions and special offers.

CAVRON-ST-MARTIN

A hamlet in the high wooded valley of the little stream, La Planquette, not far from Hesdin.

L'Estaminet chès 2 Agaches

120 route d'Aubin
Cavron St-Martin
62140 Hesdin

Tel: 03.21.81.49.16

Open every day, from 1600 – 2000.

The 2 Magpies (agache is the Picard word for magpie) is a very special place. Bruno Bachimont has a sign outside his house which says *Ebénistérie* – it is helpfully translated underneath as "Woodworks". Monsieur Bachimont is an artist in wood. He restores old classical regional furniture, or he can create faultless reproductions of any of those styles – Louis XII, Louis XIV, Regence – so beloved by the French, so baffling to most Britons. Most important of all, to my mind, he is fascinated by traditional games and has made it part of his business to rediscover and relaunch those ancient pleasures of the estaminet. Many of the revivalist estaminets in France have games provided by Bruno

Bachimont. In 1997, he opened up a bar in his showroom (with local beers, of course), so you can admire and perhaps buy, the likes of *jeu de grenouille*, *table à toupie*, or *jeu de puces*.

GRAVELINES

Gravelines is famous for its beautifully restored seventeenth century fortifications, the finest flower of Vauban's work. There are pleasant gardens, dotted with interesting sculptures, within the fortified complex. The town also has a fish smokery, a vast nuclear power station and a nationally renowned professional basketball team.

Le Queen Mary

7 place Charles Valentin
59820 Gravelines

Tel: 03.28.23.19.27

Closed Tuesday. Open 0700 – 2100 every other day of the week.

The place Valentin is Graveline's main square. Although the Queen Mary displays huge signs for Skol and Coca-Cola outside, it is more interesting than that. Long, L-shaped bar, subdued lighting, nicely furnished in very English Victorian style. Brasseurs de Gayant beers on draught, plus Pelforth. A good bottle list, including Jenlain, Trois Monts and many Belgian classics. It is billed as a "Café-Pub", which means, among other things, that you can get a beer at seven o'clock in the morning.

ST-OMER

There is a French word "flâneur", which means a stroller, a loafer, or an idler. Flâneurs will enjoy St-Omer, with its fine main square, the place du Maréchal Foch, and peripheral pedestrianised streets and alleys. The public gardens, built over the remnants of the old fortifications and beyond the vast and sombre Cathedral of Nôtre Dame, are beautiful, never more so than in autumn, as the leaves on the trees begin to turn. There are a couple of museums and, of course, the brewery, to explore. The very best of St-Omer remains hidden away from the main roads in and out of the town. The *marais audomarois*, the marshland on either side of the River Aa, is threaded with tiny canals, the *watergangs*, through wild nature and market gardens. From villages such as Tilques and Salperwick, you can hire boats and paddle and pole around this enchanting world.

La Taverne Irlandaise

11 rue Compte de Luxembourg
62500 St-Omer

Tel: 03.21.98.34.85

Open 1000 – 0100 Monday to Thursday, 1000 – 0200 Friday, Saturday and Sunday.

Down the Rue de Calais from the Grand'Place, then turn left. Opened in 1995. Irish slant comes from the tape-deck and the draught Guinness plus Kilkenny Ale. But this is a very good theatre-set version of an Edwardian *English* pub. Glossy beer menu has over eighty bottles – the usual suspects from the UK include Martins, New Castle and Gordon Finest Gold. St-Landelin, Ch'Ti's, Jenlain and 3 Monts from Northern France. My Irish friends would be highly amused to see some of the cocktails *sans alcool*. "Cork", for example, is a mixture of grapefruit and pear juice, with mint.

Don't remember that from my last visit to Cork.

Spey River Café

43 place Maréchal Foch
62500 St-Omer

Tel: 03.21.88.18.28

Open 0800 – 2400 Monday to Thursday, 0800 – 0100 Friday, Saturday and Sunday.

Huge place on the main square, packed at the weekends. Big screen TV for the football, music deafening even by French standards. The bar boasts 15 beers on draught, including Watou Blanche, Kwak, Hoegaarden. The bottled beer menu, mostly Belgian, but with 3 Monts and Pelforth, is impressive, the malt whisky list awesome.

ST-POL-SUR-TERNOISE

St-Poloise

(see brewery section).

Café de la Poste

(see brewery section).

GENIEVRE FIN D'HOULLE

Drive inland from Calais, via Ardres, towards St-Omer and you will miss the tiny village of Houlle, off to the left, by only a couple of kilometres. If you happen to be making the pilgrimage to the *Blockhaus d'Eperleques*, the ruined concrete bunker, from which German V-2 rockets were to have been launched on London, you are only five minutes away.

The Persyn Distillery is in the main street of Houlle – you can't miss it, because they have a small shop fronting the street and upon the wall above the display window, there is a plaque, placed there by the *Conseil National des Arts Culinaires*, which says that this is a *Site remarquable de goût*. The three criteria adopted by the *Conseil* are that the site should be part of the national culinary heritage, in active production: it should have aesthetic interest, from local architecture and in pleasant surroundings – and there should be a welcome for visitors. The *Distillerie Persyn* certainly fulfils all those criteria.

The distillery is small, old-fashioned and somehow much more like a farm than a factory, outside a pristine white-washed exterior. Within, there are warm brick walls, cobbled alleyways and the little River Houlle at the back. Monsieur Hughes Persyn is the perfect guide and host and displays exemplary tolerance to halting French.

The raw materials – rye, oats and malted barley – come from the surrounding countryside. Only the juniper berries, *les baies de genièvre*, used at the very end of the process, are imported, currently from the Midi and the former Yugoslavia. There are plans to change all that. They have planted a *genièvrérie*, a juniper wood, on the nearby hillside and are waiting for the trees to reach maturity. There used to be juniper trees hereabouts, and Monsieur Persyn remembers the old folk gathering the berries by snipping them into upturned umbrellas.

There are four stages in the making of *genièvre*. First, the cereals are boiled in water for about three hours. Next, the wort has a top-fermenting yeast added. After that, the resultant liquid, called for obvious reasons, *la petite bière*, is distilled, via ancient alembics, copper and conical, like wizards' hats. There are three distillations, one after the other, and only during the third are the juniper berries added – a handful are trickled into a small leather sack, and the sack is thrust through a tiny trapdoor into the still. The whole distillation process is fired by a *feu nu*, a naked (gas) flame.

The final process of maturation takes place in oak barrels, of various sizes and ages. You have to gauge time spent in old oak and new, in different sized barrels, and different vintages are blended together at the end – the end being eight months for the *Carte d'Or* (40% ABV) and four and a half years for the *Carte Noir* (49% ABV).

My first contact with *Genièvre fin de Houlle* came some time before I got round to visiting the Persyn distillery. At the end of a very sociable day with the *Arbatréliers de l'Hésdinoise* – the Hesdin cross-bow club – I was presented with a social situation involving a tableful of beers, with neat gin chasers. The beer was fine – nothing special – but the follow-up stone-cold *genièvre* had me baying for more indifferent beer, and more classy gin. "Une forte houle avec la Houlle", they said – "You get a heavy swell on with Houlle gin". A gin after a beer, or a gin *in* a beer, I subsequently discovered was part of the ancient tradition in Northern France.

A *bistouille*, in this part of the world, is a triple whammy of gin with coffee. You put a squirt of gin in the coffee, another when the coffee is half drunk, and a third mixed up with the grounds. Old timers talk of a *tricolore*, or *driekleur*, which meant that you drank a brandy, followed by a *genièvre*, then a rum. The Persyn Distillery produces a special gin mixed with crushed fruits – blackberries, blackcurrants and raspberries. A shot of that is refreshing – topped up with champagne, it is a very special treat. This latter is a sophisticated version of another old tradition, of preserving summer fruits in gin. *Genièvre* is also used in cooking – more of that later.

The work of the distillery is intimately tied up with the rhythm of the harvest, so the best time to go is from late autumn through to spring, when work is in progress and you are surrounded by the cosy aromas of steam, fermenting liquor and a haunting *soupçon* of juniper. If you would like to tour the Persyn distillery, please don't just show up at the door. It is a small family firm and they can't be expected to down tools and show you around. Make an appointment, either by telephone, fax, or by letter, a week or two in advance, and you will be made more than welcome.

Distillerie Persyn
19 route de Watten
62910 Houlle

Tel: 03.21.93.01.71

Fax: 03.21.39.25.36

BEER AND CHEESE

The cheeses of Northern France have only been recently charted, by Philippe Olivier, Maître Fromager-Affineur, of Boulogne, in his book Notre Fromages du Nord.

Monsieur Olivier is a revered figure in the complex and sophisticated world of French cheeses and his shop in Boulogne has been a place of pilgrimage for cheese lovers for many years. Here you will find an awe-inspiring selection of classic cheeses from all over the country, each and every one supplied by hand-picked top-class cheese-makers from all over France, each one, in its appropriate season, brought to a peak of perfection by conditioning in temperature – and humidity-controlled cellars – that word "affineur", or maturer, is all-important.

"France's geography", says Olivier, "is in itself the taste of the cheese". And, "cheese is a slice of French culture, as important as the historical wealth of French architecture and folklore". Life will never be quite the same once you have visited the Boulogne shop and begun an exploration of the long, winding, wonderful path among French cheeses.

So, surprising, perhaps, that Philippe Olivier has turned his considerable attention towards the cheeses of Northern France, where there is only one variety, the Maroilles, with an *appelation controlée* label? Not really, because *appelation controlée* is officialdom, whose wheels turn slowly and ponderously – and it will take time to catch up with developments in the North. Olivier is ahead of the game and already singing the praises of authentic monastic cheeses, like those of Belval, or the Mont de Cats, the old miners' cheeses, such as the *fromage fort de Béthune*, made with spices and white wine, or the cheeses of Bergues, whose rinds are carefully washed twice a week, with beer or beer yeast.

Even more important, from the beer-lover's point of view, Philippe Olivier has enlisted the aid of members of *Les Amis de la Bière*, notably Past-President and Maître-brasseur Pierre-André Dubois, to consider the infinite possibilities of matching the cheeses and the beers of the region. Beer and cheese? Why not? The best of both products are made, with local ingredients, within their regions, with tender loving care – and there are historical precedents, within the ancient monastic traditions of Northern Europe, of the manufacture and consumption of both. We are way beyond the Ploughman's lunch and the pint of bitter here.

There is a fascinating and ever-evolving debate going on, but the broad conclusions already are that the stronger and more flavoursome the cheese, the more powerful, aromatic, dark and malty the accompanying beer should be. Lighter cheeses marry well with less bitter and even slightly acid beers, selected from among the *blondes* or the *blanches*. As well as that matter of balance, there is the interesting problem of choosing a beer and a cheese from the same local area – matching products of the same *terroir*.

This list, courtesy of Pierre-André Dubois, is the beginning:

Abbaye de Belval – (a hard, uncooked cheese, rather like Port-Salut, made by the Sisters at Belval, near St-Pol). St-Poloise Grand Cru, or Ch'Ti *blonde*.

Abbaye de Mont des Cats – (hard, uncooked cheese. Contact Frère Bernard-Marie, 58270 Godewaersvelde) – Trois Monts or Goudale.

Bergues – (soft, washed rind. Try M. Ronckier, Route Moches, 59122 Killem) – La Blonde d'Esquelbecq or l'Angelus.

Boulette d'Avesnes – (cone shaped, flavoured with parsley, pepper and salt. Fromagers de

Thièrache. Monsieur Bounet, 59440 Avesnes-sur-Helpe) – Saison St-Médard or Jenlain.

Boulette de Cambrai – (a fresh, herby cheese, with chives and parsley) – l'Abbaye de Vaucelles, or Sans Culottes, or La Choulette *blonde*.

Tôme de Cambrai – (uncooked, with beer-washed rind) – la Choulette *ambrée* or Sebourg. (Both the Boulette and the Tôme de Cambrai are made by Madame Robert Sauvage, 72 Grand-rue, 59400 Seranvillers).

Crayeaux de Roncq – (soft, washed-rind cheese) – Hommelpap.

Dauphin – (from the Avesnois, and very close to Maroilles, but richer and with herbs. Usually sold in fish-shape) – La Bavaisienne or St-Landelain *ambrée*.

Fort de Béthune/de Lens – L'Atrébate *brune* or Ch'Ti *brune*.

Losange de St-Pol – St-Poloise or Réserve du Brasseur.

Maroilles – (which comes in different sizes and shapes, descending from Grand format, through Sorbais, Mignon and Quart. *La tarte au Maroilles* is a famous cheese flan) – Jenlain or Choulette *ambrée*. A well-matured Maroilles calls for a Triple Brune de St-Landelain.

Mimolette – (hard, uncooked cheese from Flanders, usually matured from 6 to 18 months) – Blanche de Lille, Amadeus or Gold Triumph. A truly mature, *vielle* Mimolette would go with Bière de Demon, Belzebuth or Trois Monts.

Pavé de Roubaix – Septante-cinq or Grain d'Orge.

Saint-Winoc – (much the same as Bergues, matured for shorter time. Contact: Madame Degraeve, 59670 Oxelaere). – l'Angelus.

Vieux Boulogne – Réserve du Brasseur or Gavroche.

Vieux Gris de Lille – (soft, washed rind. Also known as Puant de Lille, Veille Tête, so be warned. Originally a Maroilles, strong enough, heaven knows – then resalted and consumed in the mining area of Lens) – Ambre de Flandres, Pelforth Brune or Terken Brune.

Coeur d'Arras – Atrebate *ambrée*, St Patron.

Philippe Olivier
Maître Fromager-Affineur
43 rue Thiers
62200 Boulogne-sur-Mer
Tel: 03.21.31.94.74

3. LILLE

The French have borrowed the English term, weekend, with enthusiasm, and put an extra gloss on it. *Le Weekend* often means a short exploratory trip from one part of France to another to sample culture, entertainment, shopping or gastronomy – such visits are actively put together and publicised by local and regional tourist offices.

From a British point of view, *un weekend* in Lille is a very attractive and increasingly popular proposition – Lille is only a couple of hours or so and a couple of stops down the line from London these days, thanks to the Tunnel and to Eurostar. The city has everything a weekender could wish for – imposing architecture of all eras, up to yesterday, splendid restaurants, shops and markets, theatre, music, cinema, the *Furet du Nor*d, which is the largest bookshop in Europe, a cleverly pedestrianised centre and the newly and spectacularly refurbished Musée des Beaux Arts. Pay homage at Général de Gaulle's birthplace in the Rue Princesse – or the statue of Louis Pasteur, in the Place Philippe LeBon.

And then there is beer …

Breweries

Distillerie Claeyssens, Wambrechies

Jeanne D'Arc, Ronchin

Heineken, Mons-en-Baroeul

Taverne de l'Ecu, Lille

Les 3 Brasseurs, Lille

Les 3 Brasseurs, Lomme

Terken, Roubaix

Rather than list cafés, bars and restaurants in alphabetical order, I have placed them in a kind of geographical sequence, beginning, as everyone seems to do in Lille, with the Place de la Gare – the "gare" being the Lille-Flandres railway station.

Les 3 Brasseurs

(see brewery section)

La Taverne Flamande

15 place de la Gare
59000 Lille

Tel: 03.20.55.11.26

Open every day, early – 0600, until late – 0200. Food from 1000 – 0100.

A favourite haunt of British boozers, possibly because the service is more relaxed and friendly than that in the Trois Brasseurs. Basic bar, sit outside when the sun shines. Draught beers include a mix of Jupiler, Rodenbach, Guinness and Jenlain. The *bar à bières* menu is huge – over a hundred bottles, including Angelus, La Choulette, Trois Monts, Bavaisienne, Septante-Cinq. Pizzas, *flammekuches* and other fast foods.

La Palais de la Bière

14 bis place de la Gare
59860 Lille

Tel: 03.20.06.38.94

Open 0700 – 2300 every day. Saturday until 0100.

In spite of the name, not much of a palace and not especially good for *la bière*, compared with places only a stride away. They *do* offer *schmoul blouk*, a summer drink which is a mix of white wine and *bière blanche* – "blouk" would appear to be the Flemish for legless.

Au Bureau

36/38 place de la Gare
59000 Lille

Tel: 03.20.21.00.01

Open 0800 – late.

The Bureaux, now over sixty of them, all over Northern France, began with an experiment by Serge De Decker in Le Touquet in 1989. The idea was a comfortable Victorian/Edwardian-looking pub, with lots of brass, polished wood, etched-glass screens and plush velveteen-covered seating. The large and glossy standard menu/beer list has odd British overtones, but is pan-European and resembles nothing you might find in the UK. Way down in one corner of the beer list, there are three or four Northern French *bières de garde* – Angelus, Ch'Ti, Jenlain and Trois Monts.

The franchise spread quickly – this one in the Place de la Gare is number 60, another one in Lille, in the Rue Bèthune, was number 2. Each Au Bureau has a brass plate, set in the floor, telling you what number it was and what date it was opened – here there is a wall map, already out of date, indicating the spread of the franchise. The sign outside, decor inside and menu/beer list are always the same. The standing joke is that Monsieur De Decker was able to tell his wife he was "just popping down to the office" (le bureau) each time he disappeared to set up a new bar or check up on old one.

That all sounds a bit frosty – in fact this one is run by a friendly workoholic family who are well used to British invasions and cope charmingly with all problems of translation, whether concerning food, beer, or the times of the last trains.

Vinothêque Rohart

66 rue Faidherbe
59000 Lille

Tel: 03.20.06.29.92

Closed all days Sunday and *Monday morning, otherwise open 0930 – 2000.*

The Rue Faidherbe runs up from the Place de la Gare towards the Grand'Place. The Vineothêque is on the left – they usually have displays of wine in baskets on the pavement outside. An old fashioned wine merchant, with a huge selection, nicely presented and crammed agreeably into a small space. They also have almost all the best Northern French beers, plus badged glasses. The only problem is that of carrying heavy booty away – there is nowhere to park in this busy area of town.

Brasserie Jean

Place de l'Opéra
59000 Lille

Tel: 03.20.13.33.13

Open 1000 – 2400 every day.

Ground level is the cool Art Deco, piano-polluted restaurant of the swanky Hotel Carlton. In the smooth, air conditioned, basement bar, the full range of the Brasserie St-Omer beers, on draught and in bottle. A good bottle-beer list, with Ch'Ti, Jenlain, La Choulette, Trois Monts and Belgian bottles, at stratospheric prices.

125

Ah! Ca Ira

40 place due Général de
Gaulle
59800 Lille

Tel: 03.20.51.94.32

*Open 0900 – 2300 during
the week. Friday, Saturday
0930 – 0130, Sunday 1500
– 2300.* The Place Général
de Gaulle is the
Grand'Place.

A revolutionary café, one of
three in Lille, dozens
threatened throughout
France. The name is a
playful rearrangement of a
famous Revolutionary song.
In most cafés, you pay over
the odds for drinks, more so
to be served outside on the
terrace. The Ah! Ca Ira
chain seeks to change all
that, with serve-yourself,
rock-bottom all-inclusive
prices – a beer, wine,
Ricard, Scotch all at 7F, tea,
coffee, cocoa at 5F. A
"special" beer at 12F. You
can bring your own food
too. There is discernible
panic, among the
proprietors of cafés and bars
all around Lille. A pity the
beers on offer – apparently
from Interbrew, at the
moment – are fairly boring.
Now, if the managers of the
chain managed to do deals
with the regional breweries
– that *would* be a
revolution.

La Taverne de l'Ecu

(see brewery section)

Le Hochepot

6 rue du Nouveau Siècle
Lille

Tel: 03.20.54.17.59

*Closed Saturday lunch, all
day Sunday.*

Off the Rue Nationale,
not far from the Taverne
de l'Ecu, the Hochepot is
at ground level in a
modern drum of offices
and shops, dumped in a
quiet late nineteenth
century square with trees
and a fountain.

And excellent and
reasonably priced
restaurant, specialising in
regional cooking.
Monsieur Coquelot looks
like a man who enjoys his
food, wine and beer – and
he is. Local beers on
draught, in bottle, and to
take away. Recommended
by a CAMRA member
who lives and works in
Lille – lucky man.

Aux Moules

34 rue de Béthune

59000 Lille

Tel: 03.20.57.12.46

The rue de Béthune is a
pedestrianised street choc-
a-bloc with cinemas and
the likes of Marks and
Spencer and McDonalds.
Aux Moules is a good
place to take on board the
Lille prime dish of *moules-
frites*, plus a bottle of
Jenlain.

Au Bureau

52 rue de Béthune
59000 Lille

Number 2 on the Au
Bureau hit-list. Much the
same as the other one,
with identical decor and
menu/beer list. Seats
outside here.

Café Jenlain

43 place Rihour
59800 Lille

Tel: 03.20.15.14.55

*Bar open every day 1000 –
0200, restaurant 1200 –
2300, except Sunday.*

Near the Metro station in
the Place Rihour.
    Colourful, expertly
restored exterior, plain and
functional inside. Upstairs
is the *Grenier Animation
Piano Bar*, which operates
from 2100 – 0200. The
Café is the Brasserie
Duyck showcase, with
Jenlain and Sebourg on
draught (and *Bière fraîche*,
which is Sebourg
unfiltered) plus bottles.
Cuvée de Jonquilles, Trois
Monts and Bavaisienne are
available in bottle too, just
to show there are no hard
feelings towards other
regional breweries.

Cuisine à la bière includes
*Le poêlon des moules à la
bière de Jenlain,
Carbonade de boeuf à la
bière Sebourg*, etc.

La Bastringue

168 rue de Solférino
59000 Lille

Tel: 03.20.57.80.22

*Closed Monday. Open 1600
– 0200.*

The rue Solférino is a
shabby, battered boulevard
which only comes to life at
night – the whole of Lille
was like this twenty years
ago. The fish market, an
excellent adjoining fish
shop and restaurant, a lot
of Chinese restaurants –
and a litter of late night
cafés. Le Bastringue is
dark, strange, odorous,
with deafening music.
Duyck beers (Jenlain and
Sebourg). Le Queens,
opposite, has St-Omer
beers, while L'Irlandaise,
next door but one, runs
the Guinness. They are all
early-afternoon to early-
the-following-morning
joints and I am too old for
all this. Younger members
of *Les Amis de la Bière*
stress this is a good street
to play in.

Taverne du Ch'Ti

253 rue Nationale
59000 Lille

Tel: 03.20.74.82.63

*Closed Sundays. Open 1100
– late the rest of the week.*

A long walk from the
centre. If driving, note that
the Rue Nationale is one-
way, coming in to town.

An L-shaped large functional bar, mainly patronised by students from the nearby Catholic University. A Castelain house, with all the Ch'Ti range on draught, and Castelain decor everywhere, from tables to beermats. Explosive and entertaining during weekends at term time – can be deathly quiet during student vacations.

And away from the centre of Lille and into the connurbation.

Café de Paris

5 place de la République
59200 Tourcoing

Tel: 03.20.26.47.16

Open every day for lunch and evening meal, but best to book Saturday evening and Sunday lunchtime, when it can be very busy.

Not much from the outside, but cosy within. Excellent regional menu, which changes each week. Beer list of twenty or so Belgian and French beers. Very reasonable prices. Recommended by a CAMRA member, who says he dines here whenever he is in town.

La Taverne de la Bavière/PubMcEwans

143 rue Gustave Delory
59810 Lesquin

Tel: 03.20.96.06.30

Open 0930 – 2400 (closes 0100 Friday, 0200 Saturday). Pub closed Saturday lunchtime and Sunday. Restaurant closed Sunday evening.

Lesquin is south of Lille. Off the RD917 into Lille, turn into the Rue Gastave Delory (RD145); turn almost at once R into the car park.

Red brick, modern, unexciting from the outside, except for the lively and well-stocked fish merchants next door. Once inside, a pleasant one room bar, with impressive line up of twenty pumps. Draught beers are from all over the place, and include unlikely bedfellows – McEwans Scotch Ale, Hoegaarden, German beers and Bière du Desert. A couple of hundred bottled beers, many of them gathering dust as decor. A huge list of classy malt whiskies. Downstairs is a large and elegant restaurant. Although out-of-the-way, very popular. They get a lot of British customers here – escapees from the nearby Novotel, which is close to the airport. Entrepreneur Jean-Pierre Mériaux has set up many of these places, apparently with an amicable and loose deal with McEwans (ie Scottish & Newcastle, now Scottish Courage), which includes borrowing the name and occasionally stocking the beer. Several of Les Pubs McEwans are run by members of the Mériaux family, others are franchises.

La Taverne du Petit Wasquehal/Pub McEwans

2 rue Faidherbe
59290 Wasquehal

Tel: 03.20.72.02.27

Open Monday to Friday 0930 – 2400. Saturday until 0200. Sunday 0930 – 2000 – but the restaurant is closed Sunday evening.

You can only get here by car or taxi. If you are driving, it's the *voie rapide* from Lille, leaving at exit 6 for the ZI de la Pilaterie, or the A22, exit 9. The Rue Faidherbe runs off the Rue de la Couture – there is a tiny white-on-green notice pointing down the hill to the Taverne/Pub McEwans. You are very near the Heineken Brewery and it would make sense to combine visits.

Unremarkable exterior hides another Pub McEwans, with twenty draught beers (Pelforth, but otherwise mainly Belgian and German, although the selection changes), a collection of almost two hundred bottled beers and almost as many whiskies. A different featured beer of each month and seasonal delights such as the Oktoberfest, with sauerkraut and a German band. Don't try the *Fleur de bière* from Alsace, a 40% spirit distilled from beer, spiced and fruited and served in frost-covered bottle, unless someone else is driving. Beyond the bar – and on the balcony above – is the good-value restaurant, which serves food every day (bar Sunday evening) from 1200 – 2400, non-stop. Big, noisy and very popular, in spite of the difficult location. All the barmen are fast, efficient, knowledgeable – and all of them seem to speak English.

Les 3 Brasseurs, Lomme

See Brewery section.

THE GRANDE BRADERIE

In the North of France, a *braderie* can be one, or a combination of several events – a jumble sale, a flea-market, an antique fair, a second-hand or cut-price market. If it happens further south, in Picardy, they call it a *réderie*. The *braderie/réderie* is part of the regional economy which is booming – there are 2000 of them in the Nord-Pas de Calais and 600 in Picardy, each year.

The oldest, biggest and best – without doubt the granddaddy of the *braderies* – is the one that takes place in Lille over the first weekend in September. No-one really knows how old it is although some historians claim it can be traced back to the trade fairs of medieval times.

The statistics of the present-day event are mind-boggling. A hundred kilometres of city centre streets are turned into a vast pedestrianised hubbub of wheeling and dealing – two million visitors arrive to join in the fun. The *Grande Braderie* is not just a gigantic sale – it is a street festival, with rock and folk converts, and a marathon race, which ends just before the *braderie* begins on the Saturday afternoon (adding to the confusion and closing even more streets).

As befits a festival, there is traditional food and drink. The food is *moules-frites* – mussels and chips. The mussels are simmered in white wine (or beer), garlic and finely minced vegetables and are surrounded by mountains of chips. The professional way to eat mussels is to select one, eat it, then use the double-sided shell like a pair of tweezers to prize out the others. Fit the discarded shells one into the other, thus eventually forming a circle around the discard plate. The restaurants do a roaring trade and as the mussels are devoured, the shells are collected and bucketed into a heap on the pavement or in an alleyway. There is a competition to see who can build the biggest pile of mussel-debris. It is a form of advertising, of course, and the local paper dutifully publishes a picture of the winning pile (and by definition, the most popular restaurant) each year.

They say that there are records of a beer, associated with the *braderie*, back in 1446. The traditional drink these days is Jenlain, and lots of it. (The story of the conquest of Lille by the Brasserie Duyck's beer, thanks initially to the thirsty students at the Catholic University, has already been told). These days, there is competition – so much of it that one could almost claim that the *braderie* is also an unofficial beer festival. The Brasserie Castelain already has its Taverne du Ch'Ti, hopefully and strategically placed in the Rue Nationale close to the University. During the *braderie*, they also have a stall in the Place de la République, just by the Musée des Beaux Arts. The Brasserie des Amis-Réunis produced its Bière du Chamane de la Grande Braderie de Lille, in a limited edition of 2000 bottles, for the first time in 1997, while Monsieur J J Petigny offered his Bière de la Braderie de Lille (brewed in Belgium) that same year. There are also, of course, the beers from the Trois Brasseurs and the Taverne de l'Ecu, to complete the collection.

The city of the *braderie* comes to an end at midnight on the Sunday, whereupon the city of Lille has to be rescued from vast piles of litter, mountains of mussel shells, and tens of thousands of empty beer bottles. How they do it, I just do not know, but the city cleaning corps – the TRU, or *Traitment des Rejets Urbains* – spring into action and gets rid of everything inside twelve hours. The director of the TRU described the *braderie* a few years back as *un cataclysme surnaturel*. Sounds a bit dramatic to me, but then, I don't have to clear it up.

RONNY COUTTEURE
AND THE UNIVERSITY
OF BIEROLOGIE

Further education is, of course, a Good Thing – and studies at the University of Bièrologie need only take an hour or so. Bièrologie is a word you will not find in the French dictionary, but when you think about it, it doesn't need a great deal of interpretation. Ronny Coutteure offers a course in beer studies, completed painlessly and hilariously within the space of an hour or so that his cabaret act runs. You can join at any time, wherever and whenever you catch up with the performance at a small theatre, café or bar in the north of France, or even in Paris.

Monsieur Coutteure comes from Wervicq, on the River Lys, technically just across the border in Belgium, but really part of that trans-border-land called Flanders. It is more complicated than that, because Wervicq is also on the border of Flanders and Wallonia, straddling the Flemish-French language divide in Belgium. Whatever it is, this is beer country and he has fond – no, passionate – memories of the estaminets of his youth.

Many years on, and we find Ronny Coutteure as award-winning actor, writer, director and producer in theatre, television and film in France and Belgium. And then.... he goes back to his roots and sets up the University of Bièrologie.

He has astounding presence – a big man, with splendid face, wicked hooded eyes, monk-like tonsure, incredible moustache, large belly framed by violent braces. The story he has to tell is nothing more or less than the entire history, mythology and folklore of beer and brewing. There are references to and quotations from Tacitus, Asterix, Saint-Arnould, Gambrinus, Rabelais and Jacques Brel; there are folk tales, folk-sayings, poems, literary readings, songs with accordion accompaniment. Audience participation is encouraged, especially during the *dégustations* – the performance is punctuated by tutored tastings of selected beers. "If in doubt", he says, "always claim the aroma of bananas". These and other jokes are accentuated by a droop of a formidable eyelid, a twirl of the magnificent moustache, or a conclusive snap of the braces. It's funny, but deadly serious as well – Ronny is a devoted *Professeur of La culture brassicole.*

Audiences love him and at the end of the performance, there are always autograph-hunters clustered around the perspiring figure, clutching napkins, beermats and odd scraps of paper for the signature and anxious to exchange fragments of nostalgic chat about beer, breweries, estaminets – and bièrologie.

4. ARTOIS

Artois was an ancient territory, centred on Arras. The borders have varied enormously through the centuries – for present purposes, the name has been borrowed to cover an area from St-Pol and Lillers in the west to the outskirts of Douai and Cambrai in the east and border with Hainault. To the north is Flanders, to the south, Picardy.

Haut Artois, the northern section, is dominated by the *Basin Minier*, which runs through Béthune and Lens (and on into Hainualt via Douai and Valenciennes). Devastation – caused by the industry itself in its heyday, and then by its collapse and total extinction in recent times – is being worked on. The *Chaîne des Terrils* organisation toils to conserve and in some cases, transform, the old slag-heaps. Pinchonvalles, at Avion, immediately south of Lens, three-tired and one of the largest slag-heaps in Europe, is a wonder of carefully preserved strange flora and fauna. Lasnord, near Noeux-les-Mines, south of Béthune, has been turned into a dry-sky slope. There are mining museums at Bruay-la-Buissière, Harnes, Marles-les-Mines, Noeux-les-Mines and Oignies. The tourist office in Lens is offering tours of the villages and *cités* of terraced miners' housing – *les corons* – and "bed and briquet" (bed and breakfast) – in former miners' homes.

Artois, the southern part of the territory, is surprisingly rural, while Arras, a gem of a place once you get into its centre, has the feel of a country town.

The First World War haunts a central swathe through the area – a *circuit de souvenir* takes in the French National Cemetery, Notre Dame de Lorette, near Souchez and the Candadian Memorial at Vimy Ridge, among other sombre memories. Your heart will miss a beat or two.

Breweries

Annoeullin

Bécu (Fampoux)

Castelain (Bénifontaine)

AMETTES

The village of Amettes is on the D341 from Arras to Boulogne, south-west of Lillers. The road, very quiet and peaceful these days, is marked on maps as *Chaussée Brunehaut* – Queen Brunhilda was a seventh-century Merovingian monarch who oversaw the renovation and re-use of old Roman roads. After a while, these ruler-straight Roman/Brunehaut routes start to leap from the map at you – there are many of them.

Café Le Relais

1 Chaussée Brunehaut
62260 Amettes

Tel: 03.21.25.19.41

Closed Tuesday. Open 0900 – 2100.

On the main road, not in the village. Newly and nicely refurbished by the Castelain Brewery. A pleasant, spotlessly clean, quiet bar, with the full Castelain repertoire on draught. Newspapers to read and table football to play, if you are feeling energetic. Christain and Francine Dusautois used to run the McEwans III in Béthune, but came here looking for a more peaceful life. If you are British and express more than a passing interest in beer, Monsieur Dusatois will produce his autographed copy of Michael Jackson's World Guide to Beer – a souvenir of his time in Béthune, when the great man came visiting.

ANNOEULLIN

Nothing much to recommend it, except the brewery, and:

Caves d'Annoeullin

1 place Général de Gaulle
59112 Annoeullin

Tel: 03.20.85.75.31

Open 0800 – 1200, 1400 – 1930, every day except Sunday afternoon.

Hubert Murguet has a fine selection of Northern

French beer – from the Brasserie d'Annoeullin, just across the road, of course, but from other brewers as well. If you want a case of Angelus or Pastor Ale, go to the brewery, but if you only need a few bottles, this is the place. He's a wine merchant as well. All the prices are very reasonable.

ARRAS

The heart of the town was rebuilt after the First World War, in the old style, and is world famous for *Les Places* – the cobbled and arcaded *Grand'Place* and the smaller *Place de Héros*, overlooked by the fabulous Hôtel de Ville and belfry tower. Market days, Wednesdays and Saturdays, bring a country flavour into the town, with villagers offering vegetables, butter, honey and helpless small animals and birds for sale. The tourist office, in the Hôtel de Ville, offers trips up the 80 metre high belfry tower, for stupendous views, and excursions underground, into the *bôves*, or labyrinthine underground cellars below the town. These latter were heavily used by the British Army during the First World War as shelters and hospitals, then as a base for mining work towards the front line, to the west of the town – this aspect of the *bôves* system is only just being re-explored and exploited. The town giants, Colas and Jaqueline, are on static display in the foyer of the Hôtel de Ville. The Fête des Rats, at Whitsuntide, is the big town festival and Pierre Bécu, whose brewery is only a few kilometres down the road, is trying to make his St-Elixir the beer to drink.

If you arrive by car, best to leave it in the paying underground car park beneath the *Grand'Place* and explore on foot. The *Grand Place* is in fact rather bleak – head for the *Place des Héros*, surrounded by shops, cafés and bars and much more pleasant. As you enter the *Place des Héros*, note the cheese merchant's shop on the corner – his cheeses are matured in cellars below the shop and he usually has a good range of regional produce.

Taverne des Ch'Ti

17 place des Héros
62000 Arras

Tel: 03.21.23.20.38

Closed Monday, except in July and August. Open 1000 – late. Sunday 1600 – 2000.

Large one-room bar, recently renovated and refurnished à la Castelain. Drink outside on fine days. All the Castelain (and St-Poloise) beers on draught or in bottle. Snacks and fast-food. Thierry Dombrine is young, enthusiastic and shrewd – his bar is already very popular. Downstairs, in the basement, a treasure trove. "Colas and Jacqueline" is a shop stuffed from floor to ceiling with local and regional produce, including a vast selection of the very best of the Northern beers.

Estaminet des Arcades

29 place des Héros
62000 Arras

Tel: 03.21.23.07.34

Closed Sundays. Open 1000 – late.

Only a few doors away from the Taverne and a similar sort of place, if a little more comfortably customer-worn. Entertaining cartoons, of regular clients and their peculiarities, hung on the walls. Lively, with celebratory evenings – Calypso Night, Blues Night, arrival of Beaujolais Nouveau, etc. Brasserie, with *plats Flamandes*, open lunchtimes. Draught beers usually include L'Atrébate, from the

Brasserie Bécu. Cocktails include "Estaminet", which is port, gin and L'Atrébate *blonde*.

BÉNIFONTAINE

Home to the Brasserie Castelain. Backtrack from the brewery to the roundabout, turn left (remembering to go right round the roundabout, of course), past the Caves de la Tour, down the Rue Victor Hugo. Look out on the right for:

La Fontaine

58 rue Victor Hugo
62410 Bénifontaine

Tel: 03.21.69.49.49

Open 0830 – 2300 every day.

Absolutely typical French café, open-plan around the bar, with pool room and football trophies on the left, a restaurant to the right. Castelain beers on draught. Photos of the sunny south of France behind the bar – Antonio Fiormo, the proprietor, has a share in a bar near Toulon, on the Mediterranean, as well, so you may not find him here in the summer. Locals are getting used to a steadily increasing stream of foreign visitors, decanting from the brewery.

BÉTHUNE

Cloth weaving and coal mining town at various times. Still an important centre on the canal system. The Grand'Place, with restored 14th century belfry in the centre, chiming complex and pretty tunes, is a very pleasant and restful oasis. The Museum of Ethnology of the Nord-Pas de Calais will be amazing – when it is finally opened to the public sometime after the Millennium. In the meantime the staff busy themselves with superb publications on various aspects of life, past and present, in the region – such as the one on breweries and beer, listed in the bibliography.

Le McEwans III

107 place Marmottan
62400 Béthune

Tel: 03.21.01.28.16

Near the museum and the sub-prefecture. Not got round to this one, but by all accounts, it has the usual McEwans range of draught beers and whiskies, with a *cave à bières* which boasts 200 different bottles. Must be good – Michael Jackson was here. (See under Amettes).

CARVIN

You may well pass through Carvin, en route between the breweries of Castelain and Annouellin. The village is mainly dusty brick, but has an extraordinary early eighteenth century Baroque church and a quiet tradition of eighteenth century ratting. Yes, ratting, that is to say, catching rats with trained dogs and betting on the speed of the process, if a recent book on French traditional games and pastimes is to be believed. Park in the main square, which is crossed by roads in and out of town and look in one corner for:

Café de Paris

Place Jean Juarès
52220 Carvin

Tel: 03.21.77.56.20

Closed Thursday. Open 0800 until late the rest of the week.

A remarkable *cave à bières*, with over 140 on the list, some from France, the rest from all over the world, including some Russian and Israeli beers I confess I have never heard of. *Bière de feu*, or *feuebrau* is a speciality of the house. I swear I have seen a CAMRA member in here, drinking a beer which had recently been set on fire –

he said it was just the thing to settle his stomach after a rich dish of tripe we had enjoyed in a café on the other side of the square.

LENS

French friends shudder when I wax enthusiastically about Lens, which was one of the key coal-mining towns in the area known as La Gohelle. "Not a stone worth preserving in the whole place", said one of them. Well, there is the concrete railway station, built in 1928 in the shape of a locomotive, with impressive murals of workers, pits and steam trains in the booking hall. And there is the football stadium, the Stade Felix Bolaert, voted the best ground in the country for playing surface, facilities and crowd by a poll of French First Division players. *Les Sang et Or*, the (blood) Red and Golds, of Lens, are a fanatically supported team with a long proud history. I am told that beer consumption in the town doubles on winning nights.

All right, Lens is a mess, but it is a warm-hearted, lively, friendly and cosmopolitan mess, with shops and bars representing the various communities, including Belgians, Italians and Poles, who came here originally to work in the mines.

La Taverne des Ch´Ti´s

Route de Lille
62300 Len

Tel: 03.21.78.04.54

Open Monday to Friday 1000 – 1600. Friday and Saturday evenings 1900 – 0200. Sunday afternoons 1400 – 1700, for weekly Tea-Dance (!). Park in the Place Roger Salengro, or Place Cantin, and walk up the traffic-blasted Rue de Lille, La Taverne is on the left.

A handsome, if rather dimly-lit bar and good restaurant, with another room at the back for Karaoke and Tea-Dances. This was the first of the recent rash of Tavernes des Ch'Ti's. Beers on draught are therefore Castelain, plus Hoegaarden. A good bottle selection, of both beer and whisky. The restaurant specialises in Nord-Pas de Calais dishes at very reasonable prices. *Tarte à Maroilles, Croûtons de foie de volaille à la bière de Ch'Ti, Terrine de coq à la bière Ch'Ti.* Can't claim knowledge of the Karaoke or the Tea Dances.

139

McEwans

10 avenue Raoul Briquet
62300 Lens

Tel: 03.21.28.44.88

Open 0900 – 0100 during the week, 1100 – 0200 on Saturday, 1700 – 0100 Sunday.

Back towards town from the Rue de Lille, turn left into the Avenue Raoul Briquet, the McEwans is on the right.

A glittering array of pumps at the bar. Fifteen beers on draught, including Kwak, Kriek Becasse, Hoegaarden and Guinness. Around 150 bottles beers, 30 whiskies. Nice place, with compartmented seating. Football daft, with all Lens matches on big-screen TV. There's the Irish Tavern next door but one, which is trumpeted as a Traditional Irish Pub Shop – selling Kronenbourg.

Aux Délices Belges

32 avenue de 4 Septembre
62300 Lens

Tel: 03.21.70.47.42

Closed Monday and Thursday mornings. Open 0900 – 1230, 1430 – 1900. Sunday 1000 – 1300.

Back down the Route de Lille, turn right this time, past the flower shops. Aux Délices Belges is on the right.

Very smart little shop, run by the charming Madame Brigitte Merlin and specialising in Belgian chocolates and beers. 230 Belgian beers, a dozen or so from Northern France – and Newcastle Brown.

SAINTS, SINNERS AND THE BREWERS' STAR

The Brasserie Castelain has a carving of a benign St-Arnould, or Sint Arnoldus, keeping an eye on the copper in the brewhouse. They also produce their *biére sur lie*, dedicated to their Saint-Patron, who appears on the label, in jolly cartoon fashion, wearing his bishop's robes and holding a *fourquet*, the wooden fork which brewers used to stir the wort.

There are several Saints Arnouldii – two of them are held dear by European brewers and this one is Saint Arnoldus of Flanders, who is credited with stopping a plague in Bruges, c1084 AD, by plunging his staff into a brewing kettle and suggesting that people drank beer instead of water. It was a miracle and also a sensible idea, since boiling water to make beer means that waterborne germs are killed and therefore beer was safer and healthier to drink than dubious river or spring water. (Up to very recent times, in Northern France, families had beer on the table, hospitals supplied beer to patients and schools issued beer to children, for much the same reasons). Small wonder that brewers were pleased with the Saint's miraculous revelation.

The other brewers' benefactor and Patron Saint is Arnould of Lorraine. The key moment in his transfiguration can be seen dramatically portrayed in a beautiful stained-glass window, rescued from a defunct brewery, and on display at the European Beer Museum in Stenay. Arnould had been Bishop of Metz, but retired to a hermit's life, performing assorted miracles the while, somewhere in the Vosges mountains, where he died in 628 AD. His successor in Metz, one Bishop Goèric, arranged for the body to be brought back. The funeral cortège, suffering under the summer sun and the weight of the bier – and having run out of beer – ground to a halt. Goèric prayed for another miracle and lo – a pitcher of beer filled up, was poured and filled up again each time it was emptied. It was good stuff too, judging from the ecstatic expression of the customers who had drunk it, as seen in the window at Stenay. Saint Arnould, various images of whom can be seen in breweries all over Northern and Eastern France, was born near the village of Champigneulles, where the gigantic Kronenbourg Brewery now stands. So God is evidently on the side of the big battalions.

Gambrinus, or sometimes Cambrinus, is supposed to have been Duke Jean I, who lorded it over Brabant, Louvain and Antwerp in the thirteenth century. Then again, he might have been the leader of a Germanic tribe, the Gambrivii. OR … the word may come from the Latin name for the head-brewer in a mediaeval monastery, Cambarius. Cambarius is known in French as Gambière, or Cambier. The modern day *Ghilde Eswards Cervoisier*, modelled on mediaeval lines, has a *Grande Cambier* as one of its officers. Gerard Caudrelier's new micro brewery at Aubigny-au-Bac is called the Brasserie Artisinale du Cambier.

Another legend seeks to pin the name on Jean Sans Peur, Duke of Burgundy and Flanders, the founder of *L'Ordre de Houblon* in the early fifteenth century. Whoever he was, Gambrinus remains a popular iconographic figure among beer-makers and beer-tasters – portraits tend to show a plump, smiling, bearded, boozy character, a cross between Old King Cole, Father Christmas, Rabelais and Falstaff, astride a beer barrel and clutching a foaming tankard. He isn't a saint, but a harmless and entertaining sinner.

The brewers' star is more easily and convincingly explained. The ancient alchemist's signs for the four elements which combine to make the universe, and beer, – fire, water, air and earth are:

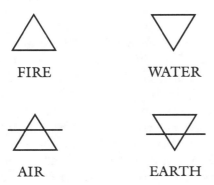

FIRE   WATER

AIR   EARTH

Put them together and what have you got?

5. HAINAULT AND L'AVESNOIS

Hainault straddles the border – there are studious arguments whether Valenciennes, in France, or Mons, in Belgium, is the capital town of the old region. The mining belt, through Douai and Valenciennes, separates the wooded and watered *Parc Naturel Régional Plaine de la Scarpe et de l'Escaut* to the north, from further countryside to the south. L'Avesnois is largely rural to the south, and takes its name from the town of Avesnes-sur-Helpe. Although there are several excellent small breweries in the northerly areas of both Hainault and L'Avesnois, cafés and bars featuring local beers are thin on the ground.

Breweries

Amis-Réunis (St-Amand-les-Eaux)

Artisinale du Cambier (Aubigny-au-Bac)

Bailleux (Gussignies)

Brasseurs de Gayant (Douai)

La Choulette (Hordain)

Duyck (Jenlain)

Entre-Temps (Valenciennes)

Theillier (Bavay)

BAVAY

A quiet town, between Valenciennes and Maubeuge, now bypassed by the N49. The Roman origins of the place are clear, as a careful look at the map will show. The straight roads radiating away from the centre used to lead to Amiens, Soissons, Reims, Cologne, Utrecht and Tournai. Many of them are now quiet country byways. A nineteenth century column in the Grand'Place commemorates Caesar Agrippa, who built the system in 26 BC, and Queen Brunhilda, who repaired it in 613 AD. German bombing during the last unpleasantness unearthed the foundations of the splendid Gallo-Roman city of Bagacum – the nine hectare site is now excavated, more or less tidied up and open to visitors and there is a modern museum full of artefacts from the explorations.

Café de Paris

Place Général de Gaulle
59570 Bavay

Tel: 03.27.63.13.05

Closed Sunday. Monday to Friday, open 0700 – 2200, Saturday 1000 – 2200.

A café-brasserie-restaurant, part of the Hôtel St-Maur, right in the centre of Bavay. A friendly place for a coffee or a beer first thing in the morning, a snack during the day, or a simple but substantial meal in the evening. The draught beers are nothing special, but they have a good bottled beer list, including Cuvée de Jonquilles and Saison St-Médard from the Brasserie Bailleux. Nothing, inexplicably, from the Brasserie Theillier, which is ten minutes walk away.

Across the road is the Café l'Amphi, which advertises *bières spéciales* and a billiard room. It has never been open when I have been in town.

CAMBRAI

A fine old town, which took a terrible battering in both World Wars. It is, however a *Ville d'Art et d'Histoire*, as of 1992, which means that the restoration of old cherished buildings has been recognised. The Museum has a brilliant *son et lumière* show, over a beautiful relief model, outlining the extraordinary history of the town. Although there are innumerable bars around and just off the impressive Grand'Place, there are none which show enthusiasm for regional beers. Things will change, I'm sure, and in the meantime, the best idea is to head for the Au Bureau, in the Place Artistide Briande.

LE CATEAU-CAMBRÉSIS

Small town between Valenciennes and St-Quentin. Known in France for the *Musée Matisse*, in the Palais Fénelon. Henri Matisse was born here in Le Cateau, and lived long enough to be present at the opening of the museum, ranked third in the various Musées Matisse in France, which contains a small but impressive collection of his drawings, engravings, paintings and sculptures. First World War buffs from Britain come to Le Cateau to inspect the site of a spoiling battle fought by the British Expeditionary Force during the long retreat from Mons, in 1914.

Le Saint Mattieu

7 place du Commandant Richiez
59360 Le Cateau

Tel: 03.27.77.06.06

Closed Sunday. Open every other day 1130 – 2400 (later at weekends, if they have customers).

Up the hill from the Matisse Museum, on the main road into the centre of town. A bikers' bar, with notice announcing "Harley parking only – Jap bikes will be crushed" and an invitation to join the Belgian Hell's Angels ("Lots of Fun"). In spite of that, a friendly place. Photographs covering the walls indicate that customers – not just bikers – have a good time here. The proprietor likes heavy rock music and plays it all the time. Interesting draught beers (including Jenlain and Guinness when I was there) – but they change from time to time. An extensive hand-written list of bottles, including L'Angelus, Bavaisienne, Ch'Ti, Grain d'Orge and Belzebuth. No-one seems to know where the John Smith's Tadcaster Ale beer towel came from.

DOUAI

A medieval *beffroi* – a bell-tower – is an essential part of a town's identity in the north of France. A town giant is a necessary part of life too. You could map out an ancient culture, straddling both sides of the border, by charting the *beffrois* and *géants*. Douai has the best-known bell-tower in the region, praised by Victor Hugo and painted by Corot, now newly restored to all its old glory and charming the hours away with various melodies from the carillon. It also lays claim to the most famous giants in the region. The three day *Fêtes de Gayant*, in early July, is among the best of all town festivals in Northern France, with concerts, processions, bicycle races and local sports, including cock-fighting, archery and the *jeu de billons*, an intricate and skilful ballet which involves throwing clubs at a target. The photographs taken by Augustin Boutique at the turn of the century and on show in an annexe of the *Musée Chartreuse*, illuminate both the town and the region. Then there is the brewery. The beer shop, mentioned in several French guides, closed a few years back, so don't waste time looking for it.

La Miroiterie Pub

66 bis rue de Lens
59500 Douai

Tel: 03.27.99.30.30

Open Monday to Friday 1145 – 1500, 1730 – 0100. Saturday 1830 – 0300. Closed Sunday.

Difficult to find. The Rue de Lens is a one-way cobbled street leading out onto the Boulevard Albert Premier. The Miroiterie was a glass and window manufacturer's, but has been transformed into the French notion of an English/Irish pub. Narrow, three floor open-plan. The absolutely magnificent bar, with Power's Irish Whiskey mirror at the back, must have been a sore loss to Dublin, whichever Irish town or city it came from. Very odd to see old adverts of Yorkshire woollen mills – Huddersfield, Honley, Linthwaite, Slaithwaite and Diggle – on the walls. Even odder to contemplate the library effect – acres of ancient books, locked and inaccessible behind glass. Closely allied to the Brasseurs de Gayant brewery and therefore stocking all their beers, on draught and in bottle. There is an encyclopaedic beer list as well.

FOURMIES

An industrial textile village, deep in the otherwise green L'Avesnois.

Saint-Louis Pub

60 rue St-Louis
59610 Fourmies

Tel: 03.27.60.04.29

Jenlain recommendation. Five draught beers, 60

plus bottles. I would like to know more.

Gussignies

Brasserie Bailleux and Café-Restaurant Au Baron (see brewery section).

IWUY

A village strung out uncomfortably along the busy N30, between Cambrai and Bouchain.

Le Robespierre

3 rue Foch
59141 Iwuy

Tel: 03.27.37.96.59

Open 0700 – 2100 every day.

Archetypal unpretentious old fashioned one-room village bar. Play table football or the pinball machine, read the Voix du Nord, contemplate the doings of the Iwuy sports teams as outlined on the noticeboard – and try one of Alain Dhaussy's La Choulette beers on draught.

JENLAIN

Come here for the beer – Jenlain is the home of the Brasserie Duyck. If you would like to try the beers on draught and in situ, try:

Les Routiers

Grand'Place
59144 Jenlain

Tel: 03.27.49.71.78

Open every day, 0800 – 2100.

Small and basic café-brasserie-restaurant, opposite the Mairie and Salle de Fêtes, on the main road into the village from the brewery. White exterior, orange tiled roof and plastered with Jenlain-Sebourg signs. Duyck beers on tap in the bar, naturally. Battered, comfortable and very much a local's place.

LEWARDE

To begin to comprehend something of the significance and the reality of the coal mining industry in northern France, you should make tracks for the village of Lewarde, a few kilometres east of Douai, down the N45. The *Centre Historique Minier* is a brilliantly realised museum archive and research centre, created on the site of the old Delloye mine, which only ceased active production in 1971. The surface buildings – offices, engine houses, lamp rooms, pit-head baths – are left, pretty much as they must have looked after the last shift. There are exhibition galleries, tracing the turbulent history of life and work in the *Bassin Minier*, with fascinating asides on miner's leisure pursuits, religious observances and political and union activities. For the guided part of the tour, you are required to don a safety helmet, ride in an open train, then "descend" into the pit itself, for an exploration of what seems like miles of tunnelling. Your guides are retired miners who actually worked the pit. They are to a man genial, humorous, knowledgeable and voluble and it doesn't matter in the least that you will understand very little of what they say, so strong are the accents. The miners liked their beer, of course, and so do you, so after the visit, you should call in at:

Le Briquet

Centre Historique Minier
Fosse Delloye
59287 Lewarde

A bar-brasserie-restaurant and souvenir shop on the museum site. An excellent range of Northern beers in bottle on offer.

The museum is open every day, except the 1st January, 15th – 31st January, 1st May, 1st November and 25th December, from 1000 – 1600 October to March and 1000 – 1700 April to September. Telephone 03.27.98.03.89.

MAUBEUGE

Once a centre of chemical and heavy engineering, very badly damaged in the Second World War. Might not sound very attractive, but it is a lively place, divided by the canalised River Sambre. In the surrounding villages, they still play La Crosse en plain, or La Choulette, around the fields in winter time.

Shakespeare

3 rue du Commerce
59600 Maubeuge

Tel: 03.27.65.14.14

Recommended by the Gault Millau/Jenlain guide. Hôtel-bar-restaurant. *Atmosphère très British*" it says. Jenlain beers for sure.

ST-AMAND-LES-EAUX

Spa and market town, north-west of Valenciennes. Brasserie des Amis-Reunis is in the former abattoir. You can visit the *Eaux minérales de Saint-Amand* establishment and watch them checking and bottling health giving spa-water – just thought I would mention it.

Le Grand Hôtel de Paris

33 Place St-Amand
(Grand'Place)
59230 St-Amand-les-Eaux

Tel: 03.27.48.21.00

Open Monday to Friday 0700 – 2200. Saturday 1000 – 2200. Bar and restaurant closed Sunday.

A comfortable, venerable hotel, a former coaching house, on the opposite side of the Grand'Place to the abbey tower. A good place to stay, to drink and to eat. On the right is the locals' corner and fast food area, to the left the more formal restaurant. They have Germinal and Jenlain on draught and an extensive beer menu, featuring other Northern French special beers and a handsome selection of Belgian bottles. The rooms upstairs are time-worn but comfortable.

SEBOURG

A holiday village in deep countryside north of Jenlain.

Le Jardin Fleuri

21 rue du Moulin
59990 Sebourg

Tel: 03.27.26.53.44

Restaurant closed all day Wednesday, and Sunday evening.

Jean-Pierre Baruzier, who runs the restaurant, was one of the chefs who helped put together the Brasserie Duyck's book of recipes (see bibliography). If your French is up to it, and he is not too busy, he has a lot of fascinating tales to tell. *Cuisine à la bière* features on his à la carte menu. Down through the pretty Japanese-style garden behind the restaurant, is the Logis de France hotel, also called Le Jardin Fleuri. Altogether a quiet and civilised place to use as a base for exploring Jenlain/Sebourg territory.

THUN ST-MARTIN

Relais Saint Hubert

3 route Nationale
59141 Thun St-Martin

Tel: 03.27.82.81.03

Open every day 0900 – 2400.

An isolated transport café, with large parking area, on the N30, north of Cambrai, just south of Iwuy. If coming from Cambrai, it is on the right. A rare outpost for draught beer from Alain Dhaussy's La Choulette brewery.

VALENCIENNES

Once a regional capital, named the "Athens of the North", then a centre of industry and coal mining. Badly damaged during the last war and recovering slowly from the end of coal. The newly restored museum is magnificent. A brand new theatre, Le Phénix, due to be opened in early 1999 in a daring and dazzling new building, the futuristic scarlet shell of which is already causing a buzz of comment.

Entre-Temps (Station buffet)

See brewery section.

Grand Hôtel de Valenciennes

8 Place de la Gare
59300 Valenciennes
Tel: 03.27.46.32.01
It *is* grand, splendidly modernised/restored in 1930s style. Elegant restaurant, included in the Gault Millau/Jenlain Guide.

BORDER HOPPING 2

Visits to the breweries Duyck, Theillier and Bailleux duly completed, give serious thought to border hopping into the Belgian province of Hainault. The road from Bavay towards Quièvrain takes you across country and across the old frontier in no time at all. It is an especially beautiful trip in springtime, when the cherry trees on either side of the road burst into blossom. There is no indication at all that you have passed from one country to the other. The Brasserie Abbaye des Rocs is on the left, opposite the turning right signposted down to the village of Montignies-sur-Roc. You won't miss the brewery – it has a huge sign, the outline of a large green bottle, erected at the side of the road. Drive into what appears to be a large ramshackle and cluttered farmyard and you have arrived.

Jeanne-Pierre Eloir used to be a tax inspector, but now he can be found wandering around, dressed in farmer's gear, scratching his head in rural fashion and affecting bewilderment at the awards and orders which keep flooding in for his beers from America. His daughter Nathalie, who is now head brewer, will be hard put to cope with all the orders. When I was there, a breathless agent in their farmhouse kitchen was trying to order beer by the pallet load for the USA; Monsieur Eloir continued to scratch his head and deal with my bill for a dozen bottles. The Eloir's beers are terrific – complex, spicy and powerful. Bring home samples of Abbaye des Rocs, Blanche des Honelles and La Montagnarde.

Brasserie Abbaye des Rocs

37 Chaussée de Brunehaut
7387 Montignies-sur-Roc
Hainault
Belgium

Tel: 065.75.99.76

Open Monday to Friday 0800 – 1800.

Only a few kilometres to the east of Montigny-sur-Roc, careful map reading will take you to the village of Blaugies. Several kilometres beyond the pleasant village centre (ask for "La Moneuse"), there is another farmhouse brewery, the Brasserie de Blaugies, opened by the Carlier-Pourtois family in 1987. Ignore the loud protestations of Sam the pony-sized St. Bernard, who may be roaming the garden, and pop into the farmhouse to ask for bottles of their Darbyste, La Moneuse and Saison d'Epeautre beers, another quite extraordinary collection. Darbyste has fig juice in it, while Epeautre is made from spelt, a highly unusual variety of wheat.

Brasserie de Blaugies

435 rue de la Frontière
7370 Blaugies
Hainault

Tel: 065.65.03.60

The Carlier-Poutois' give complicated opening times – Monday, Tuesday, Thursday, Friday 1700 – 1830. Wednesday and Saturday 0900 – 1300 – but if you make arrangements beforehand by telephone, they will sell you beer at any reasonable time.

6. PICARDY POSTSCRIPT

The *Ghilde Eswards Cervoisier*, the medieval militant arm of *Les Amis de la Bière*, are committed to protecting *Les bières des Pays Bas Français* – the "French Lowlands" being the former provinces of Flanders, Artois, Hainault and Cambrésis, the heartlands of traditional Northern French brewing and beer drinking. In other words, although they always include in their newsletter the latest information on the breweries of De Clerck, in Peronne, in the *département* of the Somme, and Bernoville, in the Aisne, Picardy, if not unknown territory, is hazily charted. (The present-day region of Picardy includes the three *départements* of Somme, Aisne and Oise).

Since, at the moment, there *are* only two breweries in the whole region, both of which rely on private customers, shop and supermarket distribution, and exports, rather than any significant spread of cafés, it is extremely difficult to list more than a handful of bars in the area. I look forward to adding to these numbers in future editions of this book.

Breweries

Bernoville (Aisonville-Bernoville)

De Clerck (Peronne)

AMIENS

A revitalised and exciting regional capital. The cathedral of Notre Dame is the main tourist attraction, as it has been for seven hundred years or so. Only a stride away from this magnificent building, across the River Somme, are the *hortillonages* – acres of market – and leisure gardens linked by tiny canals. There is a carnival and a jazz festival in May, a town festival in June, the *foire St-Jean* in June or July, a "*weekend au bord de l'eau*" (a Somme river festival) in September and an international film festival in November. The *réderies* – the Picard version of the *braderie* – are in April and October. There are countless cafés and bars, many of them, down in the district of St-Leu, with oddly anglicised names – Le Nelson, Le Queens. None of them have a significant range of regional or local beers on offer.

Chez Marius

9 rue Ernest Cauvin
80000 Amiens

Tel: 03.22.91.66.54

Open every day 1000 – 0100. Sunday 1500 – 0100.

In a pedestrianised street, handy for several of Amiens' splendid cinemas. Monsieur Delpeuch, who knows his beer, is puzzled that he can only get British beers through a Belgian agent. Thomas Hardy Ale, Samuel Smith's Strong Ale, Ruddles Barley Wine and Newcastle Brown are among the UK offerings in bottle at the moment. The six or seven draught beers are not inspiring, but the beer list is phenomenal – over 120 of them, including Colvert, Jenlain, Pastor Ale, La Choulette and Ch'Ti from Northern France. Belgian beers predominate, but there are unusual additions from Tahiti, China, Malaysia, Austria, the former Yugoslavia and Switzerland. The café spreads, cosily, over two floors. A very pleasant place, although expensive.

CAPPY

A quiet rural village by the canalised River Somme. *Le Petit Train de la Haute Somme*, a legacy of the First World War, when it was built to carry ammunition from the valley bottom to the big guns placed on the surrounding heights, huffs and puffs its way by the river near here. Tourists, and steam train buffs, flock in for the ride.

L'Escale de Cappy

22 Chaussée Leon Blum
80340 Cappy

Tel: 03.22.76.02.03

Open lunchtimes every day, but best to telephone ahead to confirm. Open Friday and Saturday for evening meal.

A small and utterly delightful restaurant, in an old stable block, originally built for horses which pulled the barges along the canal. The sign on the old stable door reads *Resteurant Ch'l'Escale a'Capin*, which tells you that Claudie Seminet is a fervent Picard. Claudie, a tiny bundle of extraordinary energy and determination, has been researching, rediscovering and refining Picard cuisine for many years now. Cooking evolves through the seasons and is firmly based on produce from the region. In the entrance hall, she sells local products, including samples of all the Picard beers from the De Clerck and Bernoville breweries.

LE HOURDEL

A tiny fishing village on the southern tip of the Somme estuary. Haunt of artists, bird-watchers and pleasure boaters.

La Point du Hourdel

(Also known as Chez Coyard)

80410 Le Hourdel

Tel: 03.22.26.61.04

Closed Tuesday. Open during the week 0930 – 2000. Weekends 0930 – 0100.

Near the lighthouse. A fishermens' pub, with tourists in the summer. A pleasantly cluttered one-room bar, decorated with bottles and nauticalia.

Draught Heineken, Pelforth and Watney's Ambrée (!), so don't bother with that. The *carte à bières*, however, is excellent, with over 100 entries, including Colvert, Jenlain, Bière du Demon. Patrice Coyard's wife does meals during the season – *moules-frites* – and exhorts customers to "try a plate of crevettes with our beer". A tiny garden with seating outside, so you can sniff the salt air and contemplate the amazing tides, sunsets and bobbing boats.

PERONNE

A large agricultural town, basically strung out along one busy street. Home to the stunning Historial, Museum of the Battle of the Somme and the First World War – and to the De Clerck brewery. The Canal du Nord, with busy barge traffic, curves around the outskirts of the town.

Café de l'Univers

3 Place Henri Audinot
80200 Peronne

Tel: 03.22.84.42.38

Open every day 0800 – 2100, later at weekends.

Bustling café, right outside the Historial. From seating outside, watch the world go by, especially on market days. Inside, bet on LOTO or the horses, watch the pool players – and try some draught Jenlain.

SAINT-QUENTIN

Take yourself off the Autoroute and climb the hill to the centre of St-Quentin. Truly astonishing and beautiful sixteenth century Flemish-style hôtel de ville in the vast Grand'Place. Collection of brilliant eighteenth century pastel portraits by Maurice Quentin De La Tour, a native son, in the Musée Antoine-Lecurer. The Canal St-Quentin winds round the bottom of the hill. The *Fêtes du Buffon* is a wild carnival at Whitsuntide, with bands from all over Europe – the *Grande Réderie et Fête de la Tripe* in September is worth going a long way to see.

Le British

2 Rue Vesoul
02100 St-Quentin

Tel: 03.23.62.67.07

Open every day 1000 – 0100.

Round the corner from the collegiate church and the Post Office. A vast café and pool/billiard/snooker hall. "Le British" because it seeks to recreate, with hilarious lack of success, a British pub. In spite of Guinness posters, fake wall plaques and redundant London taxi used as an unusual seating arrangement, this place has a wholly (young) French atmosphere. The beer list is formidable, with all the usual Northern French beers, and the rest of the world besides.

CELLAR NOTES

Resist the temptation to drink French beers as soon as you get them home. The journey will have shaken them up, probably warmed them up, and otherwise subjected them to what the Americans call "bottle shock". Store the shocked bottles upright, in a cool place, out of sunlight, and let them settle down for at least a week. Keep them in those conditions, away from the hurly-burly of life, until you decide that their time has come.

Having said that, don't let's get too precious. There is little or no point in reverentially laying down these beers, as one does with certain wines, for years. All the brewer's art has gone into providing you with a beer in perfect condition – they are brewed to be drunk as they are. This applies even to *bières de garde* – they have *already* been given their period of *garde*. A *bière sur lie* might age gracefully, but unpredictably. No-one goes around twittering about "1994 being a particularly good year, but the 1997's will be more interesting by the turn of the Millennium". The beers should have some coded indication of shelf/storage life – some brewers of country beers, like Denys Beck, will tell you to sup up within a couple of months.

Many brewers offer advice on the correct temperatures to serve their beers – take note of what they have to say. As a broad general rule, lighter bottom-fermented beers are best drunk *frais* at cellar temperature or lightly fridged (6° – 7°C). Darker ones, and top-fermented beers, should be left at room temperature for a few hours (10° – 12°C).

It goes without saying that you should serve in clean, polished and immaculate glasses, the better to enjoy the colour and behaviour of the beer. Some beers will have a matching badged and specially shaped glass. The badging apart, the notion here is not just to provide you with a collectable item, but to provide you with a glass which will best present that particular beer.

Pour carefully and slowly, because some beers can swiftly build up a riotous spilling head. If you have a *bière sur lie* on your hands, pour even more carefully, so that you do not end up with a muddy mix of beer and lees. There are different schools of thought here – some people will throw away the lees, others will add a judicious mix to the last inch or so of the glass, the stout-hearted and strong-bowelled will carefully pour the lees into a small glass and drink it off as a pick-me-up.

A couple of years back, a British supplier advertised 3 Monts as a beer voted the best of the *bière de garde* in France, by *Les Amis de la Bière*. This was puzzling, since I am a member of Les Amis, and heard nothing about this poll. A quick check revealed that no such poll had ever taken place – Les Amis consider it their duty to tenderly nurture *all* of the beers of their region, and to single out one in this way would run entirely counter to their philosophy. They were startled, and embarrassed, to find themselves so misrepresented. Nevertheless, this hustling marketing ploy, well reported in the British specialist-beer press, was subsequently faithfully reproduced in several articles and found its way into international beer guides.

Now, if you happen to be present at any of Les Amis' gatherings, where, at the end of business, they produce a selection of bottles for refreshment and contemplation, you can be sure that 3 Monts will be there, among others – it is, without question, one of the very best beers of the revival, but that is not the same thing as saying it *is* number one. These things are discussed, purely on an informal basis, but Les Amis have never committed themselves to anything remotely resembling an officially organised league table.

For these reasons, and being mindful of Les Amis' caution, I must stress that the following suggestions are mine, and no-one else's. What I have tried to do here is to suggest a couple of "cases", each of twelve bottles, which would give someone new to the beers of Northern France an idea of the range and interest of the beers available. (I am thinking here perhaps mainly of people who buy from specialist shops in Britain, or who dash into a *cave à bières* in a Northern French supermarket before catching the ferry).

The first case should provide an initial taste of the region and includes most of those most often drunk by the local connoisseurs; the second takes you a little further into the ever-developing repertoire. I have omitted those *bières de mars* and Christmas beers which are only available for limited periods and never exported. If you get the chance, try them in situ and make up your own mind. The beers are listed in *alphabetical* order.

The first case:
L'Angelus (Annoeullin)
Bavaisienne (Theiller)
Ch'Ti Blonde/Brune/Ambrée (Castelain)
La Choulette Blonde/Ambrée (La Choulette)
Colvert (De Clerck)
Cuvée de Jonquilles (Bailleux)
Goudale (Gayant)
Jenlain (Duyck)
Saison St-Médard and Cuvée de Noël – but the latter should be available all year round – (Bailleux)
Septante-cinq (Terken)
St-Patron (Castelain)
Trois Monts (St-Sylvestre)

The second case:
Abbaye de St-Landelin Triple Brune (Gayant)
L'Abbatiale de St-Amand (Amis Réunis)
L'Atrébate Blonde/Brune/Ambrée (Becu)
Belle Siska (sometimes Pot Flamand) (De Clerck)
Bière Nouvelle – sometimes Bière des Chênes – (St-Sylvestre)
Bernoville (Bernoville)
Blonde d'Esquelbecq (Thiriez)
Gavroche (St-Sylvestre)
Grain d'Orge (Jeanne d'Arc)
Hommelpap (Beck)
Sebourg (Duyck)
Tour d'Ostrévent (La Choulette)

BEER TASTING NOTES

First, some vocabulary, in case you want to describe the beer in France, to, for example, *un amateur de la bière*. Or, then again, to impress the folks back home. The words are those of Pierre-André Dubois, *maître-brasseur*, to whom many thanks. The comments are mine.

Colour – *blanche, blonde-pale, blonde-dorée, ambrée, brune-pale, rousse, brune, noire*. The last, noire/black, is used to describe stout, spelt the same, meaning the same, in English, Irish or French, but pronounced in France as "stoot". Besides colour, there is the question of clarity: *brillante, limpide, claire, louche* (cloudy), *opalescente, voilée* (hazy), *trouble*.

The head – *généreuse, crémeuse* (creamy), *dense, fine, compacte, collante* (clinging to the glass), *adhérance* (ditto), *mince* (thin), *fugace* (transient), *bulleuse* (bubbly), *instable, blanche, grisâtre* (greyish), *brunâtre* (brownish). The connoisseurs of Northern France are convinced that traditional British beer has no head at all and this worries them a great deal. Comes of only drinking beer on trips to London, I try to tell them.

Taste and aftertaste – *fraîche* (fresh, crisp), *matlée, houblonée, levurée, épicée* (spicy), *esterifée, florale, de céreales, de caramel, d'alcool, de fruit(s)*. Or, if you've picked a bad one, don't make a fuss, unless backed up by a French expert, but it could be *anormale, de rance* (rank, rancid), *de cave* (musty), *de metal, d'oxidation*.

The tasting notes which follow are *entirely* mine, and subjective in the extreme:

Brasserie des Amis-Réunis

L'ABBATIALE DE ST-AMAND

A *bière blonde*, top-fermented and re-fermented in the bottle. The addition of juniper berries – *baies de genièvre* – gives a sharp, steely flavour to the taste and finish. First appeared in 1996. 7% ABV. There has been loose talk of a "trappist-style" beer, but there is no connection with any abbey, other than the ruins and tower at St-Amand, in close proximity to the brewery. All the brewery's beers are made from Styrian Goldings, Hallertau, Tettuang and Saaz hops, plus spices, Belgian style, which include orange, coriander, aniseed, ginger and grains of paradise.

L'ECUME DES JOURS

Pale gold, top-fermented *bière sur lie*. Extraordinary stewed apple and malt aroma contrasts with clean sharp finish. 7% ABV. Both 75 and 33cl bottles are corked and wired and bear an interesting stained glass window label. This beer was orignally developed by Olivier Forrest at Evin-Malmaison in the late 1980s, then travelled with him to Brunehaut, in Belgium, then to St-Amand. The name comes by way of homage to legendary French writer, poet and jazz trumpeter, Boris Vian.

GERMINAL BLONDE

You've read the book, seen the film, now drink the beer. Pale straw coloured, with tight white head, if correctly poured. Soft malt taste wins out over very light hopping, although aftertaste is of apple. Top-fermented, filtered, sold in 33cl crown-capped bottles. Occasionally available locally on draught, when it has honey and apple finish, not at all cloying. 6.5% ABV. Tends to be served, like a lager, at too low a temperature, in both bottle and on draught.

GERMINAL AMBRÉE

Developed in late 1997. Top-fermented and filtered, like the Blonde, it is 6.5% ABV. Besides the usual hops and spices cocktail, the ambrée adds Kent Goldings hops and liquorice.

LA BIERE DU CHAMANE DE LA GRANDE BRADERIE DE LILLE

Top-fermented beer, limited edition, sold only during the Grande Braderie, where it appeared for the first time in 1997. 7% ABV. L'Ecume des Jours by another name.

Brasserie d'Annoeullin

L'ANGELUS

A classic. Pale lemon-gold, with contrasting bright white head. Faintly spicy in aroma, fresh citrus on the palette. Tends to make people cheerful, and compare it to champagne: this may be because it is considerably stronger than it tastes or looks. Perfect aperitif and/or summer drink. On draught (rarely found), it becomes, curiously, too sweet. Pale malt, 30% wheat, a top-fermented *bière de froment*. 7% ABV.

PASTOR ALE

Golden, with solid white head which clings to the sides of the glass. Faint orange in aroma, bitter orange and malt taste, long, lingering, dry finish. Top-fermented 6.4% ABV. Six weeks secondary fermentation. Made from pale malts from winter barley, and caramel malts.

Brasserie Bailleux

CUVÉE DE JONQUILLES

Universally acclaimed as one of the very best beers of the French revival. A spring beer, available all the year round. Top-fermented *bière de garde*, roughly

163

filtered with some fermentation in the bottle. Brewers' Gold from French Flanders and Hallertau hops from Germany. Rich gold, with dazzling white head. Apple and pear fruit on the palate, with some faint spice. The word moreish applies. 7% ABV.

SAISON ST-MÉDARD

The first beer from Brasserie Bailleux, a top-fermented *ambrée*, almost *rousse*, brewed for the first time on St-Médard's Day, 1989. Sweetish, soft malt and caramel, but the alcohol sings through in the strong ascerbic finish. 7% ABV.

SAISON ST-MÉDARD CUVÉE DE NOEL

Take a long and happy time comparing and contrasting with Cuvée de Jonquilles. Included here because it is available all the year round – and quite right too. This *bière de garde* is dark, oaky, spicy, with delicious late tones of coffee and chocolate. 7% ABV.

Ferme-Brasserie Beck

HOMMELPAP

Pale copper, with reddish tints. For a French beer, powerfully hopped, strong in earthy aroma and even more powerful in after-taste. Hops are Target, Magnum, Hallertau and Strisselspalt. On draught (only at the farm), it is unfiltered and even more flavoursome. Top-fermented, 7% ABV.

Brasserie Bécu

L'ATRÉBATE BLONDE

Top and triple-fermented *bière sur lie*, as are all Pierre Bécu's beers. He refuses to divulge information on hops. Golden, with ferocious white head, sometimes with flecks of yeast. At its very best, the pear and alcohol smack of Duvel. But, often inconsistent, no matter how carefully you pour. Well worth the risk, though. 6% ABV.

L'ATRÉBATE BRUNE

Deep, dark brown, with pale coffee-coloured head. Unusually refreshing ascerbic tang to it, instead of the usual rather sweet malty brown flavours popular in France. 6% ABV.

L'ATRÉBATE AMBRÉE

Apart from malts, made in exactly the same way as the other Atrébates. Malt aroma, plummy after-taste. 6% ABV.

Brasserie de Bernoville

LA BERNOVILLE

A top and triple fermented *ambrée*, non-filtered, non-pasteurised, no-holds-barred splendid beer. Extremely lively, spontaneous combustion of foam from the bottle, no matter how carefully the bottle is stored and poured. This means a dull tangerine-copper colour – *trouble* – with an ivory head. The aroma though, is a knockout of malt. Strong malt, orange and honey flavours on the palate, and a surprisingly bitter and not at all unpleasant (late) aftertaste. 7% ABV.

BIÉRE DU PAYS DE GUISE

Rich, copper-gold, with transient white head. Fresh yeast/malt aroma, refreshing fruit in the mouth, long finish. A top-fermented *bière sur lie*, pale malt, Saaz and Hallertau hops. 5.5% ABV. Splendid country beer, in crown-corked 75cl bottle.

Brasserie Artisinale de Cambier

IRIS BEER

Dull unpolished copper colour, with gigantic creamy and rocky white head. Faint malt and spice aroma, stupendous fruit – pineapple, melon – on the tongue. Disappointingly short finish. But a very good and unusual beer. Top fermented *bière de garde* and *sur lie*. That taste could be something to do with the hops – Strisselspalt, Tettnang and the mysterious "Bourgogne" – or it could be the yeast, which Monsieur Cuadrellier is equally mysterious about. Neither filtered nor pasteurised. 6% ABV.

Brasserie Castelain

CH'TI BLONDE

The standard-bearer of the Castelain range. Pale gold, with dense white head. Fruit, apple and lemon, on the palate, with extraordinary combination of sweetish malt taste and dry kick of hops on the finish. Made with three pale malts, hopped with Saaz and Northern Brewers Gold from Flanders. Fermented at low temperature, but with ale yeast. Long period, a minimum of six weeks, of secondary fermentation at low temperature, as are all Ch'Ti beers. Filtered, not pasteurised. 6.4% ABV.

CH'TI AMBRÉE

A mix of 50% pale malt, 50% Munich, aromatic and caramel malts. Hops and fermentation as for Ch'Ti Blonde. 5.4% ABV. A firm, chewy *ambrée* with spicy notes. This was the Sainsbury's *Bière de Garde*, now in some Safeways stores under its own original French label.

CH'TI BRUNE

Pale and torrified malts. Hops and fermentation as for Ch'Ti Blonde. A firm, well made beer, majestic, port-like finish. 6.4% ABV.

CH'TI TRIPLE

Malts as for Blonde. Hops ditto, with the addition of Stirrer Golding. A deceptively powerful, fruity beer, which ends with warm, full warming alcohol. 7.5% ABV.

JADE

A *bière biologique*. Spray-free pale malt. Organically grown Bio Perle and Aurora hops. Very pale watered-gold colour, with instantly disappearing white head. Soft melon and malt aroma, refreshing, zingy, citrus on the palate, dry, very brief finish. An excellent summer drink. 4.6% ABV.

ST PATRON

The St-Patron is, of course, Saint Arnould of Flanders. Pale straw-gold. A *bière sur lie* – third fermentation at warm temperature in the bottle. The yeast in the bottle is hardly noticeable. Pronounced fruit and honey flavours on the palate, sweet rich finish, with final wallop of alcohol. Deceptively strong at 7.5% ABV. A fine, dangerous, beer. Hops are Saaz, Brewers' Gold and Magnum.

KORMA

A top-fermented beer, originally brewed at the Brasserie Armand Tallende, in the Auvergne. When the brewery went bust in 1991, Yves Castelain bought the equipment, which he then re-sold to Denys Beck. The Brasserie Castelain retained the rights to the name and the recipe of Korma, a top-fermented *blonde*, at 5.6% ABV. Korma, runs the legend, is the old Celtic word meaning "barley-wine" – the word "cervoise" is a later, Gallo-Roman invention. The new Korma was released into supermarkets only, in late 1997. Saaz and Brewers' Gold hops are used.

Brasserie La Choulette

LA CHOULETTE BLONDE

For a *blonde*, the colour is going-on *ambrée*. A late summer aroma, faint malt, strong, just-harvested barley. It doesn't prepare you for the magnificent wash of caramel-toffee/malt taste on the palate, or the long, slow, burn of the aftertaste, where the hops (and yeast?) come into their own. A splendid beer. All Alain Dhaussy's beers are made from barley from the Beauce, Gatinais and Brie regions, hops from France/Flandres and Hallertau from Germany. They are top-fermented, given a month of *garde* then roughly filtered, but not pasteurised. This one is 7.5% ABV.

LA CHOULETTE AMBRÉE

This was the original back-to-the-future recipe, a former Christmas Special, reintroduced in 1981. Malts are Vienna and caramel, hops as before. Another glorious beer, this time with even stronger toffee and coffee aftertaste. 7.5% ABV.

LA CHOULETTE FRAMBOISE

A version of the Ambrée, but with natural raspberry juice added during the period of *garde*. A "beer cocktail" says Alain Dhaussy. To be drunk as an aperitif. 7% ABV.

LA BIERE DES SANS CULOTTES

Another *blonde*. 7% ABV. The balance between all these pale beers from La Choulette is very fine and all to do with the mix of bittering and aromatic hops.

LA BIERE DES SANS CULOTTES BRASSIN ROBESPIERRE

Same ingredients and strength as the *blonde* La Choulette – and very close in taste. Could be the same beer, but the label is very fine. 7.5% ABV.

L'ABBAYE DE VAUCELLES

Another blonde, going on gold, at 7.5%. Limited supplies of this splendid beer. A taste of herbs, though none are used.

LA TOUR D'OSTREVENT

Alain Dhaussy's latest creation. If you do not like this, then maybe you should give up on the beers of Northern France, and anywhere else, for that matter. La Tour d'Ostrevent is a top-fermented *bière de garde*, rich, deep-gold in colour, malt and oak aroma, full blast of malt and alcohol on the palate and a long, long, herb and more alcohol finish. Absolutely superb and should warrant an honoured place in all those (mostly American) books which rush around the world-in-eighty-beers. 8.3% ABV. And another charming label, as well.

Brasserie De Clerck

LA BELLE SISKA

The three De Clerck beers are all bottom fermented, given a period of 6 – 8 weeks garde, then filtered before bottling. La Belle Siska, aka Pot Flamand, an *ambrée*, is caramelly, but surprisingly dry. 7% ABV. Hops are Saaz, plus a bittering hop from Belgium. Monsieur De Clerck insists that all his malts must come from Picardy.

COLVERT

An interesting aromatic *blonde*, with biscuity overtones on the tongue. 7% ABV. The best selling De Clerck beer.

LA FANETTE

Another *blonde*, lighter than Colvert. The De Clerck version of a spring beer. 5.5% ABV. Rounded, smooth and refreshing.

Brasserie Duyck

JENLAIN

The best-known beer of the revival – except that Jenlain has been around since the 1930s. *Ambrée*, with reddish tint. Powerful malt and spices aroma, highly unusual taste and aftertaste – smoke, malt, fruit and spice. Very perceptive, those students in Lille who first made the beer popular. Still remarkably reasonable in price, if bought from the brewery. Money back on the 75cl bottles, too. Top-fermented. Hops are Brewers' Gold and Strisselspalt from France, Hallertau from Germany and Styrian Goldings from Slovenia. 40 days *garde*, filtered, not pasteurised. 6.5% ABV.

SEBOURG

Very pale gold, with contrasting bright-white head. Summer flowers and harvest aromas, soft citrus – orange? – on the tongue, an aftertaste to reflect upon. 6% ABV. Top fermented. Hops are similar to those of Jenlain, but used in different proportions.

LA FRAÎCHE DE L'AUNELLE

A new beer (1998) from the Brasserie Duyck and therefore a cause for celebration. La Fraîche de L'Aunelle is a *bière blonde biologique*, top-fermented and made from pale malts, with wheat and Hallertau Perle and Spalter Select spray-free hops from Germany. Honey-coloured, unfiltered and cloudy, or *trouble*. Fresh bread and honey aroma, apple and pine on the palate, and a strong clean finish. Sold in neat, clear, tiny 25cl bottles, 5.5% ABV. L'Aunelle is a stream which flows between Jenlain and Sebourg.

Entre-Temps

Top-fermented Bière de la Maison, on draught only. 5.5% ABV.

Brasseurs de Gayant

BIERE DU DÉSERT

A strong, aromatic, bottom fermented lager, usually sold in 75cl bottle, but sometimes available on draught. 7.2% ABV. The formula was changed in late 1997, to provide a "smoother" (blander?) taste.

BIERE DU DEMON

Supposed to be the strongest *blonde* in the world, when it was launched in 1982. 12% ABV.

ABBAYE DE ST-LANDELIN AMBRÉE

Top-fermented *ambrée* was the original, as brewed perhaps at the Abbey at Crespin, certainly at Rimaux, refined at Brasseurs de Gayant. Pale and caramel malts, Target, Styrian Golding, Tettnang and Strisselspalt hops. Burnished copper colour, with transient head. Strong aroma of malt, strong firm malt and fruit on the palette, fine long finish. 6.4% ABV.

ABBAYE DE ST-LANDELIN BLONDE

Technique and hops as for Ambrée. Naturally, a sharper, cleaner taste. 6% ABV.

LA TRIPLE BRUNE ST-LANDELIN

Powerful edition to the family, introduced in 1997. Top-fermented, 8% ABV. Sold in 33cl bottles only.

L'AMADEUS BLANCHE D'ABBAYE

Top-fermented wheat beer, in bottle and on draught. Refreshing undemanding summer drink. 4.5% ABV.

LA GOUDALE

Impressive screen-printed "ancient" label on the bottles, which can be large (75cl) or small (33cl). Straw-coloured, white-tight creamy head. Spring-flowers and faint malt aroma, which doesn't prepare you for the fierce, strong, but sweet flavour of malt and hop on the palette. Target, Styrian Golding and Strisselspalt hops. Nice fruit and alcohol finish. 7.2% ABV. It *is* a goud ale.

Heineken France

PELFORTH BLONDE

Bright, light, bottom-fermented, perhaps overly sweet and gassy *blonde*, difficult to avoid in Northern France. 5.8% ABV.

PELFORTH BRUNE

Strong, bottom-fermented brown ale made with pale, caramel and torrefied malts. Coppery-red brown, unusual medicinal aroma, even stranger on the tongue – malt, toffee, fruit and cough mixture. You can get used to it. Filtered and pasteurised, in bottle and on draught all over France. 6.5% ABV.

PÉLICAN

Pale lemon, Pils-type lager, in splendid litre bottles with swing-top porcelain stopper. The bottle is more memorable – and collectable – than the beer. It has been around for over 75 years, so someone must love it. 4.8% ABV.

GEORGE KILLIAN'S

Bottom-fermented "Irish Red" beer, introduced to this part of the world in 1976. 6.5% ABV.

All these "French" beers made by Heineken use Hallertau and what their Press Office calls Yakima hops. I presume they mean hops grown in Yakima Valley, in Washington State, USA.

Brasserie Jeanne D'Arc

SCOTCH TRIUMPH

A relic of the interest in British-style beers shown in France after the First World War. Scotch Triumph (6% BV) was introduced in 1936 and is still going strong. Pale and caramel malts, with a little maize, give a rich deep rub-red colour (although it is described as *brune*), while Saaz and Styrian Goldings hops provide faintly aromatic sweet flavours. Rich fruit and coffee aftertaste.

GOLD TRIUMPH

Pale gold, bottom fermented, same hops as Scotch Triumph, with the addition of Brewers' Gold. 6% ABV. Overall impression is of sweetness – caramel and sugar – with a strong, more astringent aftertaste. A curious combination. Introduced in 1984.

AMBRE DES FLANDRES

Bottom-fermented *bière de garde* (4 weeks), made with pale and caramel malts plus maize. Saaz, Styrian Goldings, Brewers' Gold hops. 6.4% ABV. Pale gold-brown, fine malt aroma, strange dry and metallic mix on the tongue, but with sweeter finish.

GRAIN D'ORGE

A top-fermented *bière de garde*, with six weeks secondary fermentation at low temperature. Pale, caramel and torrified malts, Brewers' Gold and Challenger hops – the label stresses that this is a *bière blonde des Flandres*. Gold, effervescent, with white head which vanishes quickly. Disappointingly faint malt aroma, but a positive explosion on the tongue – malt, fruit (gooseberry?) – and wicked lash of hops. Deceptively strong, at 8% ABV. This was the one which won the gold meal in its class in the USA in 1996. Not sure I understand why – it is good, but not that good, compared to the competition in Northern France.

LA BELZEBUTH

Record-breaking, strongest *blonde* in the world, they say – at 15% ABV, they may be right. A special yeast from the laboratory of University of Louvain, in Belgium, top-fermented. Copper-gold, with a fine head, which clings lovingly to the sides of the small, special, rather elegant 12.5cl glass. Strong malt aroma, slightly syrupy at first on the palate – but then a wallop of flavour, singed caramel, whisky. Long, strong, alcohol finish.

L'ORPAL PREMIERE

A new beer, introduced in 1998. It is a top-fermented blonde, at 5.6%, presented in a smart 65cl bottle. Not to be confused with:

ORPAL

Bottom-fermented, first introduced in 1949. Pale malt, some maize. Brewers' Gold, Saaz and Stynan Goldings hops. 5.2%. Orpal is very close to Gold Triumph, although it is drier and less cloying.

Brasserie de Saint-Omer

EPI DE FACON

Bottom fermented pale gold, brewed with pale malts and 20% wheat, which first appeared at the Pont-de-Briques brewery at Boulogne-sur-Mer. 5.5% ABV. Now brewed at St-Omer.

RESERVE DU BRASSEUR

First appeared in 1972, at the Brasserie du Corbeau, at Lecelles, not far from Valenciennes. It was known at this time as Reserve du Corbeau. After a series of brewery take-overs, it is now brewed at St-Omer. Bottom fermented Ambrée. 6.4% ABV.

Café de la Poste

Top-fermented La Polopolitaine on draught only. 5.5% ABV.

Moulin à Bière

LA MOULIN À BIERE
BLONDE/BRUNE/AMBRÉE

Top-fermented, fine on the day, but ludicrously expensive to take away in bottle – and desperately short-lived. The Blonde is 5.5% ABV, the Brune 6.4% ABV and the Ambrée 6% ABV.

Brasserie St Poloise

ST POLOISE BLONDE

?oloise is an out-station for the (see brewery entries). I may be I cannot tell the difference londe (from Castelain) and St th are pale-malted, hopped with rn Brewer, fermented at low temperature with ale yeast, etc. Both 6.4% ABV. Mind you, whatever the label, make no mistake, they are both high-class beers. And I may well be stupid …

ST POLOISE GRAND CRU

See above – and compare this beer with Ch'Ti Triple – what is a percentage of degrees of alcohol between friends? 7.5% ABV.

LA BLANCHE DES 7 VALLÉES

A new beer, introduced in 1998. It is a top-fermented wheat beer, on draught only at the brasserie/brewery. 5.5% ABV.

L'AMBRÉE DES 7 VALLÉS

As above, but with caramel malts added. Slightly stronger, at 5.9% ABV. It would appear that the brewery is adding its own distinctive beers to the repertoire.

Brasserie Saint-Sylvestre

BIERE NOUVELLE

This was the experimental beer that enabled the brewery to break away from the old repertoire of bottom-fermented lagers. Originally called Bière de Mars. Pale and Munich malts, with some wheat. Brewers' Gold and Hallertau hops. As always, the Ricour family stress the importance of the yeasts they use. Bière Nouvelle is similar in make-up and appearance to 3 Monts, but tastes drier. Top-fermented, a period of *garde*, non-filtered and undergoing a third fermentation in the bottle. 8% ABV. A seasonal beer, but also sold most of the year at the Brasserie Saint-Georges, Eecke, as La Bière des Chênes.

3 MONTS

One of the key beers in the Northern French revival. 3 Monts is pale gold, effervescent, with a clinging creamy-white head. Wonderful freshly-baked bread (must be the secret yeasts) on the nose, sparkles on the palate, dry, winey finish with satisfying alcohol after-burn. Life-enhancing stuff. Top-fermented, secondary fermentation at low temperature, filtered, not pasteurised. Brewers Gold (from French Flanders) and Hallertau hops. 8.5% ABV. After years of practice, still can't get used to the cork on the 75cl bottle. Also sold in Godewaersvelde as Henri le Douanier, in celebration of one of the village's carnival giants..

GAVROCHE

Latest, long-awaited offering from the Ricour family's brewery at Saint-Sylvestre-Cappel – and a stunning beer. Pale and Munich malts, top-fermented, period of *garde*, re-fermented in the bottle – be careful how you pour. Tawny-red, fine head, powerful aroma of malt and aromatic herbs, mellow fruit taste – plum? – then long aftertaste with alcohol and earthier hop. Nothing quite like it in the present range of North French beers. 8.5% ABV. Sold in new, rather elegant long-necked, crown-topped 33cl bottles. Sold as "Flanders Red Ale" in the USA.

BIERE DES TEMPLIERS

Noted in some reference books – no longer made. It sounds to me as if it might have been very close to the Bière Nouvelle.

La Taverne de L'Ecu

BIERE DE LA MAISON

The only beer so far from this new micro-brasserie. A top-fermented *bière blanche*, only on draught *sur place*. More to follow, I'm sure. 5.5% ABV.

Brasserie Terken

TERKEN BLONDE

A fine, robust, bottom fermented *blonde*. 5.2% ABV.

TERKEN BRUNE

Copper coloured bottom fermented *brune*. 6% ABV.

SEPTANTE-CINQ

An astonishing dark amber beer, made with extraordinary care and attention with half a dozen malts and several hop varieties, including Northern Brewer, Brewers' Gold, Strisselspalt, Hallertau and Tetnang. A bottom-fermented *bière de garde* (10 weeks of *garde*), filtered and pasteurised, but nevertheless retaining a riot of flavours – fruits, plum and melon, smoky malt. 7.5% ABV.

TERKEN STOUT

Greeted with great enthusiasm by *Les Amis de la Bière*, when it first appeared in 1997, this is a dark beer, made with a blend of malts including pale, caramel and torrified. Bottom fermented. Only available on draught at selected outlets. 5.2% ABV.

Brasserie Theillier

LA BAVAISIENNE

Fine coppery-gold colour, surprising since only pale malts are used. Awash with sweetish malt, but pleasantly bitter on the tongue, from the Brewers' Gold hops. Top-fermented *bière de garde*, roughly filtered before bottling. A hugely satisfying and pleasant combination. A sturdy, reliable beer – better in the large bottle, perhaps. 6.5% ABV.

Brasserie Thiriez

LA BLONDE D'ESQUELBECQ

Pale-silk gold, dazzling white head. Unusual herb-fresh aroma, smooth citrus flavours in the mouth, long dry, going-on-bitter finish. This is a top-fermented *bière sur lie*, hopped with Brewers' Gold (from Poperinge) and Saaz. A tiny scatter of the lees in the last half glass produces interesting apple flavours. 6.5% ABV.

L'AMBRÉE D'ESQUELBECQ

Introduced in 1998. Top-fermented, non-filtered, non-pasteurised. 5.9% ABV.

Les 3 Brasseurs

LES TROIS BRASSEURS
BLONDE/BRUNE/AMBRÉE

All top-fermented, "traditional" beers and all worth a try, but only available in the 3 Brasseurs. (see notes on the brewery).

LA BLANCHE DE LILLE

Pale lemon colour, slightly cloudy *bière sur lie*. Top-fermented, third fermentation in bottle. Refreshing lemony zip and extremely long finish. 7% ABV. Among the most expensive of the revival beers.

179

CUISINE A LA BIERE

The notion of cooking with beer should raise no eyebrows these days, least of all among CAMRA members. Nevertheless, some of the recipes listed here may come as a surprise, perhaps because the range of *cuisine à la bière* is so wide in Northern France. The recipes come from a variety of sources. Sometimes they have been adapted to British circumstances and the availability of ingredients. Some famous regional dishes – for example, *Potjevleesch* have been omitted, because they are far too complicated and time-consuming. Even the French tend to buy their *Potjevleesch* ready made, in a jar.

STARTERS AND SNACKS

Go to work on an egg … and a beer.

OEUFS POCHÉS À LA BIERE BLONDE

Ingredients for four:

8 eggs

One 75cl bottle of bière de garde blonde

4 slices of bread

10cl crème fraîche

20g butter

Lettuce leaves, washed and trimmed

Salt and pepper

Pour the beer into a large pan, add a pinch of salt, bring gently to the boil. Too fierce a heat and the beer will foam and climb spectacularly out of the pan. Break the eggs, one by one, into a cup, then slide each one into the boiling beer. Poach for four or five minutes, then fish them out and plunge them into a basin of cold water. Continue to boil the beer, **181** until it is reduced by half. Let it cool a little, then mix in the crème fraîche. The bread can be pan-fried in butter, or toasted and buttered. Warm up the eggs for a minute or so in the beer/crème fraîche sauce. Two eggs to a slice of toast, pour over the sauce, with added freshly ground black pepper, add the lettuce leaves.

OEUFS FRITS À LA BIERE

Ingredients for four:

4 eggs

50cl chicken stock (from a cube)

25cl bière de garde blonde

300g breadcrumbs

4 slices of bacon

25cl olive oil

Pepper

Nutmeg

Pour the chicken stock and beer into a pan. Bring to the boil. Make a roux with margarine and breadcrumbs – add the mixture gradually to it. Add freshly ground black pepper. Let it simmer. Cut bacon into thin strips, fry them in a non-stick pan, them remove and save them on a sheet of kitchen roll. Fry the eggs in the olive oil – a couple of minutes should do the trick. Add a pinch of nutmeg to the soup, then pour into four micro-waveable bowls. Add an egg to each bowl, scatter the bacon on the eggs, add another twist from the pepper mill, then zap in the microwave to reheat everything. Hot buttered toast is nice with this dish.

SOUPE À LA BIERE

There are many versions of this simple recipe. The beer that agricultural and industrial workers drank in days gone by was weak and cheap, so in a sense, this recipe using a *bière de garde*, is up-market.

Ingredients for four:

1.5 litres bière de garde blonde

1 onion 75g butter

75g flour

1 teaspoonful of sugar

Half teaspoon of ground cinnamon

150g of cream or crème fraîche

Two egg yolks (optional)

Salt and pepper

Melt the butter in a large pan. Fry the onion, gently, for seven or eight minutes. Add the flour, bit by bit, and stir continuously until you have a smooth roux. Add the beer, slowly, still stirring, then continue to simmer for 20 minutes. Add the cream or crème fraîche (and egg yolks if you are using them) and simmer for another four or five minutes. Service with slices, or fingers of toast.

SOUPE PAYSANNE

The recipe comes from Les 3 Brasseurs, the famous brew-pub in Lille.

Ingredients for six:

200g streaky or smoked bacon

200g spring greens

200g carrots

100g turnips

200g celery

100g leek

100g mushrooms

80g grated gruyère cheese

Pinch of paprika

50g butter

1.5 litres of beer brune

CUISINE A LA BIERE

1.5 litres of vegetable or chicken stock

300g grated potato

Small bunch of chervil (or chives)

Half a baguette

Salt and pepper

Cut up the bacon, rind, fat and all, into pieces. Peel and roughly chop the vegetables. Cut the baguette into slices, top each slice with grated cheese and pinch of paprika and put in the oven on a tray, under gentle heat. Put the bacon and butter into a pan; warm up under low heat, until the butter has melted. Tumble in the vegetables and let them sweat for ten minutes or so, with the pan covered. Uncover, pour in the beer, slowly and carefully, then bring to the boil, before adding the stock and grated potato. After a couple of minutes, turn down the heat and simmer for at least an hour. Add salt and pepper to taste. Serve in individual bowls. Float a piece of cheesed and paprika'd bread into each bowl. Scatter chopped chervil over the soup and bread.

POTAGE VERT

"Green" soup, the colour coming from chopped radish leaves. Part of the French tradition which says that a good cook wastes absolutely nothing. Adapted from Daniel Halstenbach's Decouvrir La Bière

Ingredients for four:

75cl vegetable, beef or chicken stock

20cl beer, preferably a Pils-type

80g pearl barley

Ground pepper and nutmeg

Finely chopped leaves from a bunch of radishes (or about the same amount of watercress).

Bring the stock to the boil, add chopped radish leaves. Allow to cool, then put through a blender.

Pour the blend into a pan, add the barley and bring to the boil. The trick here is to make sure the barley is cooked and soft – it doesn't take long. Take from the heat, add the beer, heat up again. Season with pepper and nutmeg to taste.

CHAMPIGNONS DES FLANDRES

Ingredients for two:

Small basket of mushrooms (250g)

25cl bière blonde

20g butter

100g crème fraîche

Salt and pepper

Two tablespoons grated cheese – Bergues, if you have it.

Peel and slice the mushrooms. Cook gently in butter for a couple of minutes, then add beer and continue to simmer until the mushrooms are soft. Strain the mushrooms into individual bowls. Pour the liquid back into the pan, add the crème fraîche and stir, gently reheating. Salt and pepper to taste. Pour the sauce over the mushrooms, add grated cheese. Warm up and melt cheese either under the grill or briefly in the microwave.

LE WELSH RAREBIT

Some ethnographer will some day find out why *Le Welsh* is so popular in Northern France. To add to the mystery, all their recipes are very firm about "Cheshire" cheese, whereas all British recipes say Cheddar. Even the classic Yorkshire rarebit concedes Cheddar … However, this is a splendid recipe, from the Jenlain book.

Ingredients for four:

8 thick slices of bread

80g butter

Three tablespoons of strong mustard

35cl Jenlain beer

400g grated Cheshire cheese

Salt, pepper, celery salt

Toast bread on either side. Butter one side. Melt the butter in a pan, mix in the mustard and cook gently for two or three minutes. Add 300g of the grated cheese, keep under same heat. Pour in the Jenlain. Add salt(s) and pepper to taste. Keep stirring with a wooden spoon. The idea is to obtain a thick smooth paste. Pour the rarebit on the toast, sprinkle over the rest of the grated cheese. Grill until the top of the cheese is well done and blistered brown.

CHOU-ROUGE À LA LILLOIS

Ingredients for four:

Large red cabbage

80g butter

2 onions, roughly chopped

Salt and pepper

50cl beer, ambrée or brune

Two tablespoons brown sugar

Take the tough outer leaves off the cabbage and discard them. Carve out and discard the white spines of larger leaves. Cut up the cabbage leaves into thin strips. Boil for ten minutes in lightly salted water. Drain thoroughly. Melt the butter in a large pan. Sweat the onions in the butter for ten minutes. Add the strained shredded cabbage, pour in the beer, scatter the sugar. Salt and pepper to taste. Mix everything up thoroughly. Cover the pan and cook on very low heat for an hour or more.

MAIN COURSES

A: Fish and shellfish

MOULES-FRITES

Frites are the regional snack – witness the large and splendidly decorated chip vans anchored in every town. Don't bother with the salt and vinegar – try some of the splendid array of sauces.

Moules-frites is the classic dish of Lille's Grande Braderie; traditionally accompanied by a bottle of Jenlain. Some chefs carry the logic further and include Jenlain in the recipe. The moules half of the equation is easily prepared at home – the frites are more difficult.

Ingredients for four:

1 kilogram of mussels

1 onion

1 clove of garlic (option and often not used in Northern France)

1 stick of celery

1 bouquet garni (use the tea-bag style – what the hell!)

20g butter

25 centilitres of Jenlain

Salt and pepper

Soak the mussels in cold water overnight, scrape off beards and trailing gunk.

Chop the celery and onion as finely as possible. In a large pan, heat the vegetables in the butter for a few minutes, then add the Jenlain and the bouquet garni. Bring to a gentle boil, then add the mussels and cover. Simmer for 20 minutes. The mussels should all have opened; discard any which are still closed. Drain the mussels and serve. If you are extremely sophisticated, filter the juice, pour over mussels – I don't bother to filter, but use the sauce as it is.

The frites – we are talking national chip traditions here and British chips, magnificent though they can be, will just not do for this particular dish. They are too soggy. Frites, or French fries, as American servicemen called them when they discovered them in Belgium, are cooked in a quite different way and so crunch and taste quite differently. The true experts would have you use Bintje or Rattes potatoes, peeled and narrowly chipped, fried in palm oil for five or six minutes at 160°C, then removed and dried, then replunged into the oil, this time at 180°C for another five minutes. I've heard of, but never tasted, frites fried in horse fat, with garlic.

You could make do with prepared frozen "French fried" oven chips.

POISSON POCHÉ À LA BIERE

Ingredients for four:

600g of filleted white fish (cod, hake, coley)

Stick of celery

1 tomato

1 lemon

33cl of bière blanche (wheat beer)

Salt, pepper

Chop the celery finely, quarter the tomato, slice the lemon.

Place all ingredients thus far into a pan, barely cover them with water, boil for ten minutes. Lower the temperature, add the beer, heat up again to just below boiling. Add salt and pepper. Poach the fish in this mixture for eight minutes. Remove the fish with a slotted spoon or spatula; keep the fish on warm plates. Strain the juice, then use some of it to drizzle over the fish, the rest to moisten mashed potatoes.

FILETS DE PLIE À LA BIERE

Ingredients for six:

18 small fillets of place, each one about 60g

6 shallots

75cl of bière de garde blonde

50cl of crème fraîche

150g butter

100g grated cheese (Mimolette, if you have it)

Salt and pepper

Peel and finely chop the shallots. Place them in the bottom of a buttered oven dish. Fold each fillet in two and put in a row on top of the shallots. Add salt and pepper, add the beer. The liquid should half cover the fish. Cover the dish with tinfoil and put into a hot oven for ten minutes. Remove the dish from the oven, carefully take out the plaice fillets and keep them on a warm plate under a gentle grill. Sieve the remaining juices, pour into a pan and reduce the liquid, very gently, by half. Away from heat, mix in the crème fraîche and 70g of grated cheese. Return to heat. When it is ready, pour the sauce over the fish, add a pinch of grated cheese.

TRUITE AU PAPRIKA À LA BIERE DE JENLAIN

Another excellent recipe from the Jenlain cook book.

Ingredients for four:

4 trout, each 250-300g, gutted and de-headed

3 onions, peeled and finely chopped

15cl olive oil

Level tablespoon of paprika

Teaspoon of plain flour

35cl Jenlain

1 small white cabbage, finely chopped

100g butter

Salt and pepper

Pinch of cayenne pepper

2 crushed juniper berries

250g champignons de Paris, washed and thinly sliced

Tablespoon of tomato purée

Blanch the cabbage in boiling salted water for a few minutes. Drain. Melt the butter in a large saucepan, add salt and pepper and the crushed juniper berries. Put in the cabbage and sweat it, under low heat, for 30 minutes. Heat up the olive oil in a frying pan, fry the onions, briefly, adding and stirring in the paprika and flour. Pour in the Jenlain, add the cayenne pepper and reduce the sauce by half with gentle heat. Place the trout in a buttered oven-proof dish, cover with mushrooms, add the sauce. Cook in the oven, at 200-2100C, for twenty minutes. Take out the fish with a slotted spoon, keep them warm. Put the remaining juices in a pan, add tomato purée, stir well and reduce by half again. Pour the sauce over the fish and serve.

B. Meat and Poultry

CARBONADE FLAMANDE

You can get involved in many arguments about what constitutes an "authentic" carbonade – do you use cheaper, tougher cuts, which older folk undoubtedly did, or do you go for steak, as sophisticated chefs tend to do? This recipe, an amalgam of several, offers a simple version of the classic dish.

Ingredients for six:

1.5 kilogrammes of cubed beef; chuck steak or shoulder

100g lard

3 tablespoons plain flour

3 tablespoons wine vinegar

3 tablespoons brown sugar

1 litre beer (*ambrée* or *brune*)

50cl water

300g onions, peeled and finely sliced

Pinch of thyme and 4 bay leaves

2 cloves

Salt and pepper

In a large frying pan, brown the meat, salted and peppered, in lard. Add the onion. Scatter flour in melted butter in another pan, stirring the while to make a roux. Add wine vinegar, stir, then pour in beer and water. Five minutes later, add sugar, herbs and cloves, salt and pepper. Cook for another ten minutes. In an oven proof casserole dish, pour this mixture over the meat, cover and simmer under low heat for three hours. The sauce should be thick and going on treacly. If it is still thin separate out and reduce.

CIVET DE LAPIN À LA BIERE

Ingredients for four:

A rabbit, skinned, de-gutted and cut into pieces

50g butter

2 onions, peeled, chopped and thinly sliced

Bouquet garni

2 cloves

Salt, pepper and mustard

25cl bière brune or stout

25cl water

Sweat the onion in butter in a large pan. Add the rabbit pieces and brown. Add bouquet garni, cloves, salt and pepper. Mix a tablespoonful of mustard in

191

luke-warm water, and add. Cook slowly for an hour, pour in the beer and cook for another half hour.

COQ À LA BIERE

A grandfather (or, more likely, grandmother) peasant dish, usually enjoyed after the melancholy day when the old cock died. The chances of finding an old cock are pretty remote – use chicken pieces. The original recipe, here somewhat simplified, came from Claudie Seminet, at L'Escale de Cappy, by the River Somme.

Ingredients for six:

1 large chicken, or cock, cut into pieces

2 bottles (of 75cl) bière rousse or blonde

Tablespoon of brown sugar

Tablespoon of strong mustard

2 onions, peeled and finely sliced

4 shallots, ditto

1 clove garlic, ditto

2 carrots, ditto

1 leek, ditto

1 stick of celery, sliced

Salt and pepper

Pinch of thyme, 3 bay leaves

50g lard or butter

Brown the pieces of chicken in 30g lard or butter, in a frying pan. Put in a casserole, add salt, pepper, herbs and beer. Let it marinate all night. Next morning, cook onions, shallots, carrots, leek and celery in 20g lard or butter, in a pan for 10 minutes. Add sugar, mustard and the beer from the marinade. Mix well, cook another 10 minutes. Everything now goes back into the casserole and is cooked in gentle heat for 2 to 3 hours. Fish out the chicken pieces and keep them warm. Pass the sauce through a sieve. In a large pan, make a roux of butter and flour, pour in the sauce, mix up well. Add the chicken pieces and mix and warm.

PORC À LA BIERE

Ingredients for six:

1 kilogramme of loin chops (or, even better, cubed pork steak)

50g butter

500g peeled and sliced onions

Bouquet garni

75cl of bière de garde blonde

Slice of bread

Tablespoon mustard

Tablespoon plain flour

Salt and pepper

Brown the chops in 25g butter. Lift out, then sweat the onions in the same pan with the rest of the butter. In a buttered ovenproof dish, put alternate layers of pork and onions, with the bouquet garni in the middle. Pour in the beer, which should almost cover the meat and onions. Smear both sides of the bread with mustard, put the slice on top of the mix. Cover the casserole and cook slowly, on gentle heat, for three hours. Take out the meat. Put all remaining juices, and the bread, through the blender, reheat, then pour over the meat.

BOEUF À LA BIERE

Ingredients for six:

1 kilogramme cubed beef

37cl Jenlain

2 peeled and thinly sliced onions

10cl olive or vegetable oil

2 tablespoons plain flour

1 tablespoon mustard

8 small peeled tomatoes

Springs of thyme

Salt and pepper

Rub the beef with thyme, place in dish, pour over the beer and marinade for at least eight hours. Drain and save the liquid, roll pieces of beef in flour. In a large saucepan, sweat the onions in the oil for five minutes, then add the beef. Add salt and pepper. Brown the beef, mix in the mustard and cook a little longer. Pour in the marinade, then let simmer for an hour or more. Add the tomatoes for the last ten minutes.

POULARD DE LICQUES

Licques, in the Pas-de-Calais, near Ardres, is famous for poultry rearing. The last weekend before Christmas, they have their Turkey festival, when troops of the unfortunate birds are paraded through the village, to great rejoicing. Their recently deceased brethren are already on sale, in the shape of turkey sandwiches.

Ingredients for four:

1 poulard, cut into pieces (a poulard is a fattened chicken)

200g streaked or smoked bacon, cut into small strips

2 tablespoons oil

20cl chicken stock

20cl genièvre

25cl crème fraîche

40g butter

Salt and pepper

Marinade:

2 carrots

2 onions

1 stick celery

1 bouquet garni

8 juniper berries

1 litre bière de garde ambrée

Peel and thinly slice vegetables for the marinade. Leave the chicken pieces in the marinade overnight. Brown the chicken pieces in oil with bacon in a frying pan. Remove and place in casserole. Cook the vegetables from the marinade in butter five minutes, then place them with the chicken in the casserole. Pour in the beer from the marinade, the genièvre and chicken stock. Cover and cook at medium temperature for 40 minutes. Take out the chicken pieces and keep warm. In a pan, reduce the cooking juices, strain, then put back in the pan and add and mix in crème fraîche. (The sauce can, if you wish, be enriched with two egg yolks and lemon juice). Serve chicken pieces, pour over sauce.

C. Desserts

TARTE À LA BIERE

An enormously popular dessert in the North – a sort of beer-custard flan.

The paté sucrée (rich pastry base):

300g butter

100g caster sugar

150g ground almonds

4 eggs

450g plain flour

Pinch of salt

Pinch of bicarbonate of soda

150g brown sugar

The filling:

3 eggs

50/75cl bière de garde ambrée or brune (volume of beer depends upon size and depth of the flan-ring).

Knob of butter

The idle way out is to buy a pre-cooked short-crust pastry case. Otherwise – put the flour in a bowl. Add pinches of salt and bicarb. Make a hole in the middle, add the thoroughly beaten eggs, the sugar and ground almonds. The butter which is cut up into small pieces, is scattered into the flour. Knead the mixture together with your fingers, working the flour and butter into the liquid centre. When it is thoroughly kneaded and soft, roll up into a ball, put into a plastic bag and leave somewhere cool for several hours. Roll out the mixture on a floured board. Line a 22cm flan ring with the pastry, trimming the edges. Sprinkle the brown sugar in the bottom of the pastry case, and bake in a pre-heated oven at 200°C for forty minutes.

The filling is made by mixing up the beaten eggs with a knob of butter and beer. Fill the pastry case, cover with tinfoil, bake at the same temperature for 15 minutes. Take out of the oven, let it cool to room temperature. Tarte à la bière can be eaten warm or cold.

PAIN PERDU, AVEC CREME À LA BIERE

Pain perdu is, literally, "lost bread". French bread – real French bread – goes stale fairly quickly, but there is always a use for it.

Ingredients for four:

4 thick slices of stale bread

2 eggs

20cl milk

100g butter

20g caster sugar

For the sauce:

25cl cream

75cl beer – L'Angelus

20 egg yolks

200g vanilla sugar

Soak the bread in milk, then dip in beaten egg and sugar mixture. Fry in butter. Beat the egg yolks and sugar in a large bowl. Pour the beer into a saucepan, add the cream, bring to the boil. Take off the heat, pour a third of the mixture into the bowl of beaten eggs, stirring vigorously. Empty the contents of the bowl back into the pan. Warm up the sauce, but don't let it boil. Pour sauce over the pain perdu.

CREPES

Beer pancakes.

Ingredients for four:

400g plain flour

4 eggs

75cl beer

2 tablespoons melted butter

Pinch of salt

Cinnamon

Put the flour, with pinch of salt, in a bowl. Make a hole in the centre, pour in beaten eggs, add the beer, stir well into a smooth thin paste. Make the pancakes in the usual way, in a frying pan with butter. Flavour each crêpe with a pinch of cinnamon.

TRAVEL AND ACCOMMODATION

Getting there:

The opening of the Tunnel caused ferocious competition and spectacular price cutting between ferry operators. Chaotic – but good news for consumers. I have a friend who, wanting to travel to France with his car, took the trouble to phone all the operators, in the summer of 1997; he got wildly differing non-book price quotes, and an offer from one company to undercut the lowest price he had obtained from anyone else. This panic stricken and therefore totally acceptable face of Capitalism may be a thing of the past – companies have merged, services rationalised, therefore prices are liable to remain stable. It is still worth shopping around, or asking a travel agent to do this on your behalf. There are some incredible bargains to be had, if you book ahead, go for the five day return option, or go out of season.

Eurostar Tel: 0345 881 881
London (Waterloo)/Ashford/Calais/Lille express

A wonderful experience, apart from anything else. Foot passengers only, of course. The train trundles decorously through Kent and the Tunnel, then hurtles through France at 300 kilometres an hour. The French enjoy pointing out the contrast. Waterloo to Lille is 2 hours, Ashford to Lille, one hour. (Remember the time difference between England and France when you make your calculations.) The buffet, in keeping with long standing British tradition, is expensive and not especially good.

 Telephone service on this number is, alas, appalling – always engaged or rings out without reply. Let your travel agent take the strain.

Hoverspeed Tel: 0990 240 241. Fax: 01304 240088
(Dover-Calais, Folkestone-Boulogne)

Hovercraft, on the Dover-Calais route takes 35 minutes, SeaCat 50 minutes. The SeaCat from Folkestone to Boulogne takes 55 minutes.

Le Shuttle Tel: 0990 353 535

The French wanted to call it La Navette, but the name Le Shuttle prevailed. Put yourself and the car on the train – Folkestone to Coquelles/Calais, in 35 minutes. A dream ticket – once you have managed to get the ticket. Best to deal through a travel agent. In spite of all those adverts, featuring satellite close-up photographs of French villages and extolling the undoubted virtues of the service, the basic contact number is permanently engaged, even in the off-season.

P & O European Ferries Tel: 0990 980 980

Internet: http://www.poef.com
(Dover-Calais, Hull-Zeebrugge)

Dover-Calais is 75 minutes.

The Hull-Zeebrugge service is truly excellent for anyone travelling from Scotland, the Midlands or the North of England. Only one boat a day, a fourteen hour overnight crossing. Zeebrugge to Lille is an hour or less by car along the Autoroutes. Just bear in mind that Lille is signposted in Flemish – Rijsl – almost all the way through Belgium.

Holyman Sally Ferries Tel: 0990 595 522

Fax: 01843 589 329
Internet: http://www.holyman-sally.com
(Ramsgate-Ostend)

A keenly priced and efficient service – ie cheap and cheerful. The high-speed catamaran takes less than two hours, while the traditional ferry takes four hours. Ostend to Lille is 48 miles, all by fast

Autoroutes. A terrible shame they stopped the Ramsgate-Dunkerque service. Dunkerque now has no ferry service at all and many shop keepers, restaurateurs and café owners are distraught.

SeaFrance Tel: 0990 711 711
Internet: http://www.seafrance.com
(Dover-Calais)

The only French company operating a cross-Channel service. Crossing time is 90 minutes. SeaFrance claim they will match any price offered by other operators on single, five day, or period returns.

Stena Line Tel: 0990 707 070
(Dover-Calais, Newhaven-Dieppe)

Dover-Calais is 90 minutes by Superferry. Newhaven-Dieppe takes 2 hours 15 minutes by the Stena Lynx catamaran, 4 hours by "traditional" ferry. Dieppe is some way south from beer territory.

Staying there

CAMPING

Campsites in France vary enormously. The cream of the crop, carefully inspected and graded, are included in the annual *Michelin Camping and Caravanning Guide,* which has an English language introduction to enable you to decipher the coded entries. Perfectly good sites sometimes slip out of the guide – Camping Le Vert Bocage, behind the wonderful Taverne Flamande, in Millam, near Watten, is a case in point. (Telephone the Taverne for prices and reservations.) If you have the time, it is worth consulting the local tourist office in the area which interests you.

BED AND BREAKFAST

The bible is *Chambres & Tables d'Hôtes,* published by Gîtes de France each year. Chambres d'hôtes means bed and breakfast – if the entry in the guide says tables d'hôtes, it means your hosts provide optional evening meals as well. The classic beer-lover's example would be Madame Peugniez's chambre d'hôte in Fampoux, a working farm which is directly opposite the Brasserie Bécu. She doesn't provide evening meals, but will direct you to the Café des Sports, in the village, which is an education in itself. Most chambres d'hôtes are interesting because your hosts know what's what in the region, although it helps to speak at least basic French. These days, there are several English language guides to selected chambre d'hôtes, with selections winnowed from the main list.

HOTELS

The essential publication is the annual *Logis de France Guide des Hotel-Restaurants.* The Logis are a chain of almost 4000 individually-owned, mostly comparatively small hotels. A multi-lingual introduction helps you to disentangle the entries in the guide, including prices. It is worth looking out for the ones which display the Menu de Terroir symbol, where you can expect to find food from the region, very reasonably priced. Excellent examples of Logis de France hotels would be Le Jardin Fleuri, in Sebourg, just north of Jenlain and the Duyck brewery, and the Hostellerie des Remparts in Peronne, five minutes' stroll from the De Clerck brewery.

Most of the Logis de France hotels are reasonably priced. You can pitch lower, by calling in to local tourist offices, or higher, by consulting annual guides such as Gault-Millau, the Michelin red guide, or European edition of the Good Hotel Guide.

TELEPHONES

Telephone numbers in the North of France are all ten digits, the first two of which are 03. If, for example, you are already in France and you want to ring Fabrice Gaudé, to fix up a tour of the Brasserie

Castelain in Bénifontaine, the number is 03.21.08.68.68. To telephone from Great Britain, you prefix 00.33, then omit the first zero on the French number, thus the number you want is 00.33.3.21.08.68.68.

To telephone home from France, you dial 00.44, omit the first zero of the home STD code, then dial the rest.

Most French telephones these days take *télécartes*, which you can buy from newsagents and tobacconists. These cards give you a certain number of *unités*, or credits; the illuminated display in the kiosk will tell you how many credits you have used and how many you have left. They are much more of a bargain than a BT charge card. There is an additional bonus, if you are interested in such things – French *télécartes* are pleasingly designed and the designs change frequently. Old cards become "collectibles", and are swopped or sold on French second-hand markets, in much the same way as are old stamps or vintage postcards.

In country areas, you may find that the telephone boxes will not take cards, but only coins.

NAVIGATION

The best map to plan from is the Institut Géographique National (IGN) Tourist Map Number 101 "Pays du Nord, Picardie". For finer detail, when you are tracking down breweries or cafés in country areas, you will need the larger scale Série Verte IGN maps, Numbers 1(Abbeville-Calais), 2(Lille-Dunkerque), 3(Rouen-Abbeville), 4(Laon-Arras), and 5(Charleville-Mezieres-Maubeuge).

Useful addresses:

LES AMIS DE LA BIERE

Membership currently costs 120FF per year; for this you get the Gazette, a modest desk-top production, which, besides articles on beer and breweries, contains news of meetings, events and trips. Meetings are free, unless there is a meal involved. There is usually a small fee for trips. The big bonus is the ticket to the presentation of Christmas beers. Les Amis have recently signed up their 1000th member, although only a quarter of those could be said to be active. There are a handful of British members.

You *cannot* join the Ghilde des Eswards Cervoisiers – you have to be asked. If you are invited, you then have to be *intronised*, which is not as painful as it sounds. You are dressed up in the robes and paraphernalia and have to swear to defend beer – in particular the beer of Northern France – before the assembled company of Eswards and Amis. They give you a script to read from and it is all great fun.

Write (in French, of course) to:

Monsieur Louis Peugniez
Président
Les Amis de la Bière
"Moulin le Compte"
62120 Aire sur la Lys
France

Tel and Fax: 03.21.39.14.52

GAMBRINUS FRANCE

Le Club de Collectioneurs d'objets de service de brasseries – the collectors of breweriana. This is a national organisation, which organises meetings (often in breweries or beer museums) and sales and swop fairs. There is a quarterly magazine, *La Tegesto Gazette*, which is full of erudite stuff on the changing pattern of logos on beer tins, plus fascinating information on vanished breweries and the opening of new micro-breweries. Membership costs 150FF (190FF if paying by Eurocheque from abroad).

Write for application form to:

Gambrinus France
18 Avenue de Lattre de Tassigny
92360 Meudon la Forêt
France

or telephone 01.46.32.88.51

LA MUSÉE EUROPÉEN DE LA BIERE

The museum is housed within an imposing building which began life in the 17th Century as a quartermaster's store within the fortifications of this old border town. From 1875 until the First World War, it was a malthouse, supplying about fifty local brewers – after that there was a slow decline into coal-store, mushroom factory and occasional military prison. It was rescued from dereliction by local enthusiasts, the idea of a museum of brewing was born, some help was forthcoming from the region and the state and the place opened in 1984. Today, the museum welcomes 32000 visitors a year.

It is a truly fascinating place, packed with exhibits ranging from mash-tuns, coppers and fermenting tanks down to bottle-tops and ash-trays, rescued from defunct breweries all over France. Allow at least two hours to take it all in – and the entrance money (currently 28F) includes a free beer in the cellar-bar afterwards.

Serious beer-buffs, researchers and students are invited to work in the nearby *Centre de Documentation*, where there are archives of over a hundred breweries, plus thousands of photographs. There is a library of books and periodicals. Work here must be pre-arranged with the Curator of the whole enterprise, Philippe Voluer. Monsieur Voluer is a world-renowned historian of beers and breweries – he is also extremely welcoming, friendly and helpful.

Musée européen de la Bière
Rue de la Citadelle
55790 Stenay

Tel: 03.29.80.68.78

Fax: 03.29.80.31.11

The museum is open every day 10-12, 14-18, from 1st March to 20th November. Outside the season, open only by prior arrangements.

The museum, together with the *Conseil Régional de Lorraine*, have put together a booklet, *La Route de la Bière* – a tour of the once brewery/beer rich area. Unfortunately, apart from the massive Kronenbourg plant at Champigneulles and a handful of recently opened micros, the tour is largely for industrial archaeologists – all the breweries are derelict.

Regional Tourist Information

COMITÉ REGIONAL DE TOURISME NORD-PAS DE CALAIS

Useful for general tourist information on the region. Ask for the annual Nord-Pas de Calais Découvert (with useful map), or booklets on camping, hotels and fêtes.

CRT Nord-Pas de Calais
6 place Mendès France
59800 Lille

Tel: 03.20.14.57.57

Fax: 03.20.14.57.58

DEPARTMENTAL TOURIST INFORMATION

Comité Départemental de Tourisme du Nord
6 rue Gauthier de Chatillon
BP 1232
59013 Lille Cedex

Tel: 03.20.57.59.59

Fax: 03.20.57.52.70

COMITÉ DÉPARTEMENTAL DE TOURISME DU PAS DE CALAIS

24 rue Désille
BP279
62204 Boulogne-sur-Mer

Tel: 03.21.83.32.59

BIBLIOGRAPHY

Brasseurs de France: Bière et Mer. Collection of recipes for sea food and beer matching and cooking, by three world-class chefs. Handsome booklet produced in 1996, by the French Brewers' Association.

Brasserie Duyck: 52 Recettes à la Bière. Produced by the brewery in 1995. Available at Jenlain.

Colin, Jean-Claude: Agenda de la Bière 1998. A desk-top diary, brilliantly presented, packed with sometimes whimsical information on beer world-wide, produced for the first time in 1997, by Imag'In. A splendid idea, but a personal grouch; Britain is obviously at the end of the known universe, so the relevant entries are often hilariously inaccurate – Roger Protz, revered beer writer of our time, becomes Roger Prost (a relative of a certain French racing driver?), while Guinness is described as a Winter special drink. *Les Bières Britanniques*, a list of British brewers, has to be seen to be believed. There are just 16 of them, but it does say "Etc" at the end.

Colin, Jean Claude: Voyage au bout de la Bière (Guide Gourmand de la Bière), Schortgen, Luxembourg 1997. A scatter-gun list of breweries, bars and restaurants throughout France and the rest of the beer drinking world. Not much more than a list of names, with no addresses. Often inaccurate.

Coutteure Ronny; Initiation à la Bièrologie; le Temps de la bière. La Voix du Nord 1997. If you don't manage to make one of Ronny Coutteure's lectures/cabaret acts, then you could treat this book as a do-it-yourself course in "bièrologie".

Deulin, Charles: Contes d'un Buveur de Bière. La Découvrance Editions, Rennes 1995. Collection of

208

fantastical boozy stories, first published in 1868, now reprinted. Individual members of Les Amis de la Bière seem to know the stories by heart, especially the one about Gambrinus, Roi de Bière.

Dubois, Duronsoy, Van Bost: Nord-Pas de Calais, terre de brasseries. Document d'Ethnographie Regional No 9. Musée d'Ethnologie Régionale, Béthune, 1998. Latest in a magnificent series of monographs of life in the north, this one with contributions from retired master-brewer and Past-President of *Les Amis de la Bière*, Pierre-André Dubois and ethnographical researchers Nathalie Duronsoy and Nathalie Van Bost.

Halstenbach, Daniel: Découvrez la Bière. Editions SAEP, Colmar 1997. Very basic stuff, nicely presented, by another Alsace-based writer. Interesting recipes.

Havet, Yves: Le Houblon de Flandre Française. Menschen Lyk Wyder, Godewaersvelde 1987. History of hops in French Flanders.

Hernandez, Jean-Pierre: Cafés Dunkerquois. Editions Kim, Rosendael-Lez-Dunkerque 1993. Splendid nostalgic crawl around the bars of Dunkirk.

Jackson, Michael: Michael Jackson's Beer Companion. Mitchell Beazley 1993. The section on Bière de garde is pp 139-145.

Jackson, Michael, Ed: The World Guide to Beer. The Apple Press 1997. Section on France pp 179-183.

Lebey, Claude, Ed. L'Inventaire du patrimoine culinaire de la France: Nord-Pas de Calais. Albin Michel 1992. Excellent compilation of local produce and traditional recipes.

Lees, Graham and Myers, Benjamin: The Encyclopaedia of World Beers. Colour Library Direct 1997. French section is pp118 – 119.

BIBLIOGRAPHY

Loosen, Michel, Ed: Estaminets et Jeux de Flandre. Foyer Culturel de l'Houtland, Steenvoorde 1993. A hefty compilation of memories, lovingly collected and edited by Michel Loosen.

Messiant, Jacques: Estaminets des Pays du Nord. Flandres-Hazebrouck, 1996. A massive, sprawling, profusely illustrated work, expensive but worth every centime. Everyone who has written about estaminets has been inspired by this book. That includes me.

Protz, Roger: The Ultimate Encyclopaedia of Beer. Carlton Books 1995. Section on France pp 57-63.

Szczesniak, Grégiore: Brasseurs et Bières en Nord. Laura Editions, Cuincy 1996. Good general introduction to the breweries of the North, although it seems to rely heavily on brewery publicity hand-outs, rather than personal experience. Nicely illustrated.

Van Bost, Nathalie: Brasseries en Cambrésis. Itineraires du Patrimoine, 1994. Beautifully produced booklet with splendid colour photography, encouraging a tour around a host of old defunct brewery buildings in the area around Cambrai. Tempting, but I prefer my breweries alive and still brewing.

Voluer, Philippe: Stenay – La musée europeen de la Bière. Citedis Editions, Paris 1997. Short, excellent guide to brewing history and to the museum, as you would expect from Philippe Voluer.

Voluer, Philippe: Petite et Grande Histoire de la Bière de Mars. Musée européen de la Bière. ND. All you need to know.

Voleur, Philippe: La Savoureuse Histoire de la Bière de Mars. Association des Brasseurs de France 1994. A shorter and snazzier version of the above.

Von Tromp, Simon: Tromp's Beer Traveller in West Flanders. Published by the author, Second edition,

1997, covers French Flanders in more detail than the first. An enthusiastic and excellent guide to both sides of the border. Available from the author, at 25 Ranville, Carlton Colville, Lowestoft, NR33 8UB. £3.30 including postage.

Woods, John and Wrigley, Keith: The Beers of Wallonia. The Artisan Press 1996. The definitive guide to the breweries and beers of the French speaking area of Belgium. An instant classic, from the first day of publication. Essential for border hopping from Hainault (France) into Hainault (Belgium).

Ronny COUTTEURE

INITIATION
À LA BIÈROLOGIE

LE TEMPS
DE LA BIÈRE

LA VOIX DU NORD

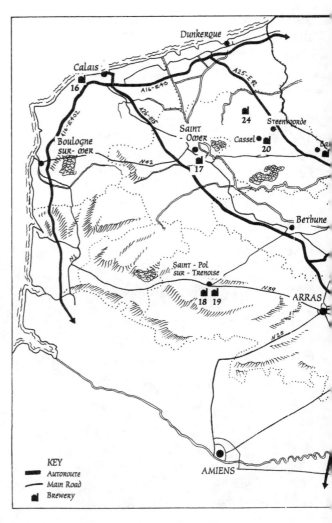

KEY TO MAP

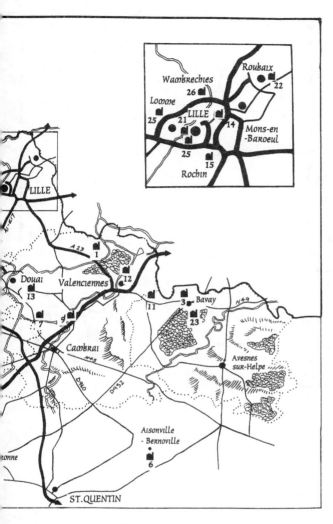

I/We wish to join the Campaign for Real Ale and agree to abide by the Rules.

Name(s)
....

Address
....

....

....

Postcode
....

Signature   Date
....

I/We enclose the remittance for:

Single:	£14 ☐	Joint	£17 ☐	(at same address)
OAP Single	£8 ☐	OAP Joint	£11 ☐	(at same address)
Unemployed/Disabled £8 ☐				
Under 26	£8 ☐	date of birth		

For Life and Overseas ratees please contact
CAMRA HQ (tel: 01727 867201)

Send your remittance (payable to CAMRA) to:
The Membership Secretary, CAMRA,
230 Hatfield Road, St Albans, Herts., AL1 4LW

Instruction to your Bank or Building Society to pay by Direct Debit

Please fill in the whole form using a ball point pen and send it to:

Campaign for Real
Ale Ltd,
230 Hatfield Road,
St. Albans,
Herts
AL1 4LW

Originator's Identification Number

| 9 | 2 | 6 | 1 | 2 | 9 |

Reference Number

| | | | | | | | | | | | | | | |

FOR CAMRA OFFICIAL USE ONLY
This is not part of the instruction to your Bank or Building Society

Membership Number

Name

Postcode

Name of Account Holder(s)

Bank/Building Society account number

| | | | | | | | |

Branch Sort Code

| | | | | |

Name and full postal address of your Bank or Building Society

To The Manager	Bank/Building Society
Address	
Postcode	

Instructions to your Bank or Building Society
Please pay CAMRA Direct Debits from the account detailed on this instruction subject to the safeguards assured by the Direct Debit Guarantee. I understand that this instruction may remain with CAMRA and, if so, will be passed electronically to my Bank/Building Society

Signature(s)

Date

Banks and Building Societies may not accept Direct Debit instructions for some types of account

✂ -

This guarantee should be detached and retained by the Payer. the Payeeee

The Direct Debit Guarantee

■ This Guarantee is offered by all Banks and Building Societies that take part in the Direct Debit Scheme. The efficiency and security of the Scheme is monited and protected by your own Bank or Building Society.

■ If the amounts to be paid or the payment dates change CAMRA will notify you 10 working days in advance of your account being debited or as otherwise agreed.

■ If an error is made by CAMRA or your Bank or Building Society, you are guaranteed a full and immediate refund from your branch of the amount paid.

■ You can cancel a Direct Debit at any time by writing to your Bank or Building Society. Please also send a copy of your letter to us.

The CAMRA Books range of guides helps you search out the best in beer (and cider) and brew it at home too!

Buying in the UK

All our books are available through bookshops in the UK. If you can't find a book, simply order it from your bookshop using the ISBN number, title and author details given below. CAMRA members should refer to their regular monthly newspaper What's Brewing for the latest details and member special offers. CAMRA books are also available by mail-order (postage free) from: CAMRA Books, 230 Hatfield Road, St Albans, Herts, AL1 4LW. Cheques made payable to CAMRA Ltd. Telephone your credit card order on 01727 867201.

Buying outside the UK

CAMRA books are also sold in many book and beer outlets in the USA and other English-speaking countries. If you have trouble locating a particular book, use the details below to order by mail or fax (+44 1727 867670).

Carriage of £3.00 per book (Europe) and £6.00 per book (US, Australia, New Zealand and other overseas) is charged.

UK Booksellers

Call CAMRA Books for distribution details and book list. CAMRA Books are listed on all major CD-ROM book lists and on our Internet site: http://www.camra.org.uk

Overseas Booksellers

Call or fax CAMRA Books for details of local distributors.

Distributors are required for some English language territories. Rights enquiries (for non-English language editions) should be addressed to the managing editor.Good Beer Guides

These are comprehensive guides researched by professional beer writers and CAMRA enthusiasts. Use these guides to find the best beer on your travels or to plan your itinerary for the finest drinking. Travel and accommodation information, plus maps, help you on your way and there's plenty to read about the history of brewing, the beer styles and the local cuisine to back up the entries for bars and beverages.

These are comprehensive guides researched by professional beer writers and CAMRA enthusiasts. Use these guides to find the best beer on your travels or to plan your itinerary for the finest drinking. Travel and accommodation information, plus maps, help you on your way and there's plenty to read about the history of brewing, the beer styles and the local cuisine to back up the entries for bars and beverages.

Good Beer Guide to Munich and Bavaria

by Graham Lees

206 pages   Price: £8.99

A fifth of the world's breweries – some 750 – are located in the region covered by this guide. The beers have rich, deep flavours and aromas and are generously hopped. You will find dark lagers, wheat beers, members of the ale family, wonderfully quenching and refreshing beers that have become cult drinks. The guide tells you where to find the best beers and the many splendid bars, beer halls and gardens, and the food to match. You'll also find all the background information for the world's most famous beer extravaganza, the Munich Oktoberfest.

Author Graham Lees, a founder member of CAMRA, has lived and worked in Munich for several years and has endlessly toured Bavaria in search of the perfect pint.

Use the following code to order this book from your bookshop:
ISBN 1-85249-114-0

Good Beer Guide to Belgium, Holland and Luxembourg

by Tim Webb

286 pages   Price: £9.99

Discover the stunning range and variety of beers available in the Low Countries, our even nearer neighbours via Le Tunnel. There are such revered styles as Trappist Ales, fruit beers, wheat beers and the lambic and gueuze specialities made by the centuries-old method of spontaneous fermentation.

Channel-hopping Tim Webb's latest edition of the guide offers even more bars in which an incredible array of beers can be enjoyed. If you are going on holiday to this region then you'll find details of travel, accommodation, food, beer museums, brewery visits and festivals, as well as guides to the cafés, beer shops and warehouses you can visit. There are maps, tasting notes, beer style guide and a beers index to complete the most comprehensive companion to drinking with your Belgian and Dutch hosts.

Use the following code to order this book from your bookshop:
ISBN 1-85249-139-6

Good Beer Guide

edited by Jon Preece

546 pages   Price: £10.99

Fancy a pint? Let CAMRA's Good Beer Guide lead the way. Revised each year to include around 5,000 great pubs serving excellent ale – country pubs, town pubs and pubs by the sea.

The guide includes information about meals, accommodation, family rooms, no-smoking areas and much more.

Fully and freshly researched by members of the Campaign for Real Ale, real enthusiasts who use the pubs week in, week out. No payment is ever taken for inclusion. The guide has location maps for each county and you can read full details of all Britain's breweries (big and small) and the ales they produce, including tasting notes.

CAMRA's Good Beer Guide is still Britain's best value pub guide – a must for anyone who loves beer and pubs.

Known Gems & Hidden Treasures
A Pocket Guide to the Pubs of London

by Peter Haydon

224 pages   Price: £7.99

If you live in or visit London, then you need this guide in your top pocket! It will take you to the well-known and historic pubs you must not miss, but also to the pubs which are tucked away and which locals keep to themselves.

The grass roots organisation of CAMRA and beer journalist Peter Haydon have brought London's pubs alive through their descriptions of ale, food, entertainment, history and architecture. These pubs have a story to tell.

The pubs in this pocket, portable, guide are listed by locality with a street address and London postal code districts heading pages so that you can easily match your location with the nearest pub. The guide covers pubs which are near tube and railway stations and gives relevant bus route numbers. It covers central London out to the commuter belts of Bushey and Surbiton.

Use the following code to order this book from your bookshop: ISBN 1-85249-118-3

CAMRA Guides

Painstakingly researched and checked, these guides are the leaders in their field, bringing you to the door of pubs which serve real ale and more...

Good Pub Food

by Susan Nowak

448 pages   Price: £9.99

The pubs in these pages serve food as original and exciting as anything available in far more expensive restaurants. And, as well as the exotic and unusual, you will find landlords and landladies serving simple, nourishing pub fare such as a genuine ploughman's lunch or a steak and kidney pudding.

You'll discover cooking from a new wave of young chefs who would prefer to run a pub than a restaurant. Many pubs are producing the traditional dishes of their regions, building smokeries, keeping cattle and goats, growing vegetables and herbs, creating vibrant, modern cuisine from fresh ingredients. Recipes from some of them are dotted about this guide so you can try them at home.

Award-winning food and beer writer Susan Nowak, who has travelled the country to complete this fourth edition of the guide, says that 'eating out' started in British inns and taverns and this guide is a contribution to an appreciation of all that is best in British food...and real cask conditioned ale.

Use the following code to order this book from your bookshop: ISBN 1-85249-116-7

Room at the Inn

by Jill Adam

242 pages   Price: £8.99

From the first pub claiming to have sold Stilton cheese to travellers in 1720 to old smugglers haunts in Dorset, Room at the Inn gives details of pubs up and down the country offering generous hospitality. Travellers and tourists looking for a traditional British alternative to bland impersonal hotels need look no further than this guide.

The guide contains almost 350 inns – plus some hotels and motels – which provide overnight accommodation and a wholesome English breakfast. Some have been welcoming visitors for centuries. You'll also find a good pint of real ale on your arrival. To help you further there are maps, information on pub meals, family facilities, local tourist attractions and much more. Room at the Inn is a must for the glove compartment of the family car and vital reading for anyone planning a bed and breakfast break, sports tour or business trip.

Use the following code to order this book from your bookshop:
ISBN 1-85249-119-1

Real Cider Guide

by Ted Bruning

256 pages   Price: £7.99

Cider is making a major comeback and Real Cider is worth seeking out wherever you are. This guide helps you find one of Britain's oldest, tastiest and most fascinating drinks. Cider has been made in Britain since before Roman times. But most cider you find in pubs today has been pasteurised, with carbon dioxide added. The resulting drink bears little resemblance to the full-flavoured taste of traditional Real Cider.

Reading this guide makes your mouth water as you leaf through details of more than 2000 pubs selling the real stuff. There are also many farmhouse producers from all over the country and outlets for Cider's equally drinkable cousin, Perry – if you bring a container. Some will even sell you a container! Author Ted Bruning is the editor of the Cider Press, a quarterly supplement to What's Brewing, CAMRA's national newspaper. He has collated information from all over the UK to give you a taste of this fine traditional drink. So why not join him and savour a wealth of different flavours?

Use the following code to order this book from your bookshop:
ISBN 1-85249-121-3

Pubs for Families

by David Perrot

256 pages   Price: £8.99

Traditional pubs with CAMRA-approved ale and a warm welcome for the kids! Nothing could be better. But where to find such a hospitable hostel on home patch, let alone when out and about or on holiday? This guide is the adult answer to your eating and drinking requirements, with facilities for your children too! Invaluable national coverage with easy to use symbols so that you know what facilities are available and regional maps so you'll know how to get there. Get the best of both worlds.

Use the following code to order this book from your bookshop: ISBN 1-85249-141-8

50 Great Pub Crawls

by Barrie Pepper

256 pages   Price: £9.99

Visit the beer trails of the UK, from town centre walks, to hikes and bikes and a crawl on a train on which the pubs are even sited on your side of the track!

Barrie Pepper, with contributions and recommendations from CAMRA branches, has compiled a 'must do' list of pub crawls, with easy to use colour maps to guide you, notes on architecture, history and brewing tradition to entertain you. All you have to do is to move your legs and arms! A great way to discover the pubs of Britain. Use it well and we'll make it the first of a series.

Use the following code to order this book from your bookshop: ISBN 1-85249-142-6

Brew Your Own

Learn the basics of brewing real ales at home from the experts. And then move on to more ambitious recipes which imitate well-loved ales from the UK and Europe.

Brew your own Real Ale at Home

by Graham Wheeler and Roger Protz

194 pages   Price: £8.99

This book is a treasure chest for all real ale fans and home brew enthusiasts. It contains recipes which allow you to replicate some famous cask-conditioned beers at home or to customise brews to your own particular taste. The authors have examined the ingredients and brewing styles of well-known ales and have gleaned important information from brewers, with and without their co-operation. Computer-aided guesswork and an expert palate have filled in the gaps where the brewers would reveal no more.

As well as the recipes, the brewing process is explained along with the equipment required, all of which allows you to brew beer using wholly natural ingredients. Detailed recipes and instructions are given along with tasting notes for each ale. Conversion details are given so that the measurements can be used world-wide.

Use the following code to order this book from your bookshop: ISBN 1-85249-138-8

Brew Classic European Beers at Home

by Graham Wheeler and Roger Protz

196 pages   Price: £8.99

Keen home brewers can now recreate some of the world's classic beers. In your own home you can brew superb pale ales, milds, porters, stouts, Pilsners, Alt, Kolsch, Trappist, wheat beers, sour beers, even the astonishing fruit lambics of Belgium... and many more.

Graham Wheeler and his computer have teamed up with Roger Protz and his unrivalled knowledge of brewing and beer styles. Use the detailed recipes and information about ingredients to imitate the cream of international beers. Discover the role played by ingredients, yeasts and brewing equipment and procedure in these well-known drinks. Measurements are given in UK, US and European units, emphasising the truly international scope of the beer styles within.

Use the following code to order this book from your bookshop: ISBN 1-85249-117-5

Abbaye de Vaucelles

Bière de P...

BERNOVILLE

75 cl   5,5% vol

FERMENTATION HAUTE

BIÈRE

...RASSÉE EN FLANDRE
DE SAIN...

BRASSERIE BÉCU FONDÉE EN 1862

Cette bière,
100% malt, a été fabriquée
suivant les traditions ancestrales.
La troisième fermentation en bouteille
garantit une bière brassée avec passion.

L'ATRÉBATE

BIÈRE BLONDE de TRADITION

Depuis
1862

75 cl Cat.5

6% ALC. VOL.
EMB. AF 62119 FAMPOUX

LA CHOUL...

Frambo...

BIÈRE SPÉCIALE AROMATISÉE À L...
Brassée et embouteillée...
Prodotta e imbottigliata dalla...
Beer brewed and bottled...
BRASSERIE LA CHOULETTE S.A. 59111 N...

6,2%vol

A consommare de préférence avant fin/ Da consumarsi prefe...

Saison Saint Medard

7% Vol. alc   75 cl.

BIÈRE DE NOËL

Brassée selon les méthodes traditionnelles avec les malts et les houblons les plus réputés et sans
produits chimiques Non filtrée, refermentée en bouteille, cette bière doit être servie fraîche (10-12°C)
et vendue avec précaution. DÉCANTER, CONSERVER VERTICALE.

BRASSERIE BAILLEUX - CAFÉ & RESTAURANT AU BARON 59570 GUSSIGNIES • TÉL : 03 27 66 88 61

...avroche

Fermentation
Haute
SPECIALITE
BIÈRE SUR LIE

...RASSERIE DE SAINT SYLVESTRE (FLANDRE)   33 cl

SEBOURG

Bière de garde blonde

BRASSÉE À JENLAIN EN AVESNOIS • NORD

224